10

for **Identifying Neglect**

Pat Beesley

BAAF
ADOPTION
& FOSTERING

Published by
British Association for Adoption & Fostering
(BAAF)
Saffron House
6-10 Kirby Street
London EC1N 8TS
www.baaf.org.uk

Charity registration 275689 (England and Wales)
and SC039337 (Scotland)

© BAAF, 2011

British Library Cataloguing in Publication Data
A catalogue record for this book is available from the British Library

ISBN 978 1 907585 18 0

Project management by Jo Francis, BAAF
Designed by Helen Joubert Design
Typeset by Jonathan Harley
Printed in Great Britain by TJ International

Trade distribution by Turnaround Publisher Services, Unit 3, Olympia
Trading Estate, Coburg Road, London N22 6TZ

BAAF is the leading UK-wide membership organisation for all those
concerned with adoption, fostering and child care issues.

Contents

Introduction **1**

Tip 1: Examine the context in which you are working **4**

Tip 2: Learn the lessons from serious case reviews **18**

Tip 3: Recognise when a child is being neglected **28**

Tip 4: Listen to the child **42**

Tip 5: Understand the impact of neglect on children **56**

Tip 6: Understand why parents neglect their children and identify signs of risk **68**

Tip 7: Consider different components of the assessment **79**

Tip 8: Recognise when children in public care are suffering neglect **100**

Tip 9: Use interventions effectively **111**

Tip 10: Know when enough is enough **123**

Afterword **132**

Bibliography **133**

This series

Ten Top Tips for Identifying Neglect is the ninth title in BAAF's *Ten Top Tips* series. This series tackles some fundamental issues in the area of adoption and fostering with the aim of presenting them in a quick reference format. Previous titles are:

- *Ten Top Tips for Placing Children*, by Hedi Argent
- *Ten Top Tips for Managing Contact*, by Henrietta Bond
- *Ten Top Tips for Finding Families*, by Jennifer Cousins
- *Ten Top Tips for Placing Siblings*, by Hedi Argent
- *Ten Top Tips for Preparing Care Leavers*, by Henrietta Bond
- *Ten Top Tips for Making Introductions*, by Lindsey Dunbar
- *Ten Top Tips for Supporting Kinship Placements*, by Hedi Argent
- *Ten Top Tips for Supporting Adopters*, by Jeanne Kaniuk

Details are available on www.baaf.org.uk.

Acknowledgements

Special thanks to colleagues in BAAF and to the children and young people and all those practitioners in children's social care, education and health who have contributed to my understanding of the impact of neglect on children's lives. Thanks also to Shaila Shah and Jo Francis for their editorial skills and helping me keep on track, and to BS for being a critical reader.

Note about the author

Pat Beesley worked for BAAF for more than 12 years as a consultant and trainer. Her professional background includes social work in a range of settings, with many years as a practitioner and manager in adoption and fostering. She is the author of *Making Good Assessments*, a resource guide for social workers assessing adopters and foster carers; BAAF's Practice Note on *Assessing Second Time Adopters*; the pamphlet *Thinking of Joining a Fostering Panel?*; and co-author of *Preparing to Adopt*, a training programme for prospective adoptive parents. She is retired and works occasionally as an independent social worker.

Introduction

To include the topic of child neglect in a series on Ten Top Tips may appear somewhat anomalous. Child neglect is a hugely complex area of work and a publication of this size cannot cover everything you need to know about the subject. Instead, the aim of this book is to provide guidelines on identifying and responding to neglect for frontline practitioners working with children and families. There are other well-known and highly commended texts on child neglect that will give you a deeper understanding of the subject. Familiarity with supporting legislation, your agencies' policies, procedures and practice guidance will also underpin your practice in this area.

Neglect can have a serious and long-lasting effect on children's development both in the short and long term, and its consequences can be far more pervasive than other forms of maltreatment. And yet there are still failures to intervene in situations of child neglect. This often reflects the complex and multi-faceted nature of neglect and the fact that most children who are neglected live in families whose lives are disorganised, complicated and overwhelmingly difficult.

This book is based on a set of principles underpinning good practice in working with neglect:

- the welfare of the child is paramount;
- the child's voice must be heard;

- identification and intervention in child neglect can only be achieved successfully through multi-agency working; and
- the child's welfare depends on practitioners working to agreed thresholds for intervention.

The recent increase in care proceedings in the UK, in the wake of the death of Peter Connolly (Haringey, 2010 (DfE, 2010a)) and other child deaths, serves as a reminder of the extent of child neglect. It has, for some time, been the category most used when deciding whether a child should have a child protection plan, and it is a common theme in serious case reviews. It is a complex area of safeguarding with practitioners struggling to determine when and in what circumstances signs of neglect meet the threshold for intervention. The result of this can be desensitisation, tolerance of unacceptable standards of parenting and the failure to notice the child lost in the middle. At the same time, there is an already overburdened care system struggling to cope with an increase in looked after children.

In most cases, neglect is an ongoing and pervasive experience with cumulative effects. It is not like an incident of physical abuse where there are often clear signs that lead to definitive action. Being able to identify and respond to neglect relies on collecting and interpreting a range of evidence and making sense of it. Individual workers will make their own interpretations. If you are working with neglect, reflective practice and good supervision are essential tools. You will be faced regularly with examining your own values and beliefs about parenting and child care practice. Without an opportunity to reflect on the meaning of what you see and how you react, you may miss or become inured to critical signs and indicators that could make a difference to a child's life. Reflective practice should be part of day-to-day work.

Recent overview reports of serious case reviews (Brandon *et al*, 2008, 2009; Rose and Barnes, 2008) have highlighted key areas of practice that need to be improved to prevent serious maltreatment of children. These include:

- better identification and reporting of signs of abuse;
- a focus on the child's lived experience;
- addressing meaningfully issues of diversity;
- better case recording;

- improved communication and collaboration between practitioners involved with the child and family; this should include practitioners in adult services;
- a better understanding of the impact on children's health and development of parental substance misuse, mental illness, learning disability and domestic violence;
- improved in-depth assessment, including better analysis and reflection, enhanced by good management and supervision.

This book reflects these important areas of practice. It will help you to consider your role in working with neglect cases, and reflect on the messages from serious case reviews and their application to practice. It will help you to understand the impact of neglect on children,* understand why some parents neglect their children, and also to consider how you might intervene to improve children's lives.

This book is written primarily for children's social care practitioners, but it will also be relevant to practitioners working with children and families in other disciplines. The focus of much of this publication is on the imperative of multi-disciplinary working, without which we risk failing large numbers of children.

---

* Within this text, the term "children" is used to refer to children and young people, unless referring to a specific group.

TIP 1

Examine the context in which you are working

Inevitably, your practice is shaped by your personal and professional experiences and the context within which you work. To be a competent and confident practitioner, you need an awareness of and insight into the many factors which can influence policy and practice. This chapter addresses some of the factors which set the context for working in the area of child neglect. In the wake of high profile child abuse scandals, this is a difficult time for anyone involved in the field of safeguarding and child protection,* particularly social workers, whose profession seems to be continually under the spotlight.

---

* The term "safeguarding" refers to protecting children from harm, preventing impairment to their health or development, and ensuring that they are growing up in circumstances which provide safe and effective care with optimum life chances. The term "child protection" is the process of protecting individual children identified as suffering, or likely to suffer, significant harm from abuse or neglect.

However, it is to be hoped that these high profile cases raise our awareness and concern for neglected children and lead to improved practice.

Consider the impact of your personal and professional experience

Your own experiences of growing up will have helped to shape you into the adult and, for some, the parent you are today. Each person's experience of family life will be unique. Some will have been lucky enough to have experienced a loving, secure and stable home; others may have suffered neglect or abuse themselves as children. Some will not have wanted for anything materially, others may come from families where every penny counted and material possessions were few and far between. Whatever your individual experiences, they will in some way colour the meaning you give to parenting and the impact that children's lives have on you. You will have developed ideas of what you believe constitutes good parenting. This will be shaped by a range of factors – culture, family life, ethnicity, class and the religious or spiritual values you hold.

> *We all have our skeletons and I am no different, I just have to be aware of what's influencing what I am doing … There will always be potential triggers – abuse has a lifelong impact so it's important to have a strong supportive network around to be able to reflect openly about the work you are doing.*
>
> *(Social worker with personal experience of neglect as a child)*

Other influences will include the particular perspective of your profession, the organisational structures you work within, your knowledge and professional experience and your accumulating practice wisdom. The views and opinions of colleagues, managers, practitioners from other disciplines, and the particular theoretical frameworks that you apply to your understanding of children's lives are all factors in the equation.

Reflecting on the impact of personal and professional experiences and different perspectives on understanding children's needs will help in this work. It might be useful to consider the following questions.

- What does "parenting capacity" mean to me?
- Does it mean the same to my colleagues?
- Where does my understanding of "good enough"* parenting come from?
- What is my understanding of what children need from family life?
- What does the term "child neglect" mean to me?
- How will I know neglect when I see it?

Consider the impact of professional and ethical values when working with neglect

Safeguarding practice is underpinned by both international and national legislation, regulations and guidance, as well as your respective professional codes of ethics or practice.

Summary of key aspects of the UN Convention on the Rights of the Child (UNCRC):

- The child's welfare is paramount.
- Treat children and families with respect, honesty and care.
- Listen to children, take what they have to say seriously and act on it in an appropriate manner.
- Obtain the wishes and feelings of the child where possible/ practicable.
- Work in partnership with families but acknowledge appropriate power differentials and responsibilities.
- Recognise that sometimes it will be necessary to act against parents' wishes where the child is at risk.
- Remember all children and the families in which they live are different. Consider their different needs and experiences according to their racial and cultural heritage, language, religion, gender, sexuality, age and any physical or learning disability.

---

* It is important not to confuse the concept of "good enough" parenting with parenting that is just about acceptable. "Good enough" parenting, according to Donald Winnicott (1958), acknowledges the difficulty in being the perfect parent and allows for some failure in the overall context of meeting the child's needs.

- Adopt an anti-discriminatory approach and practice.
- Focus on the strengths of the family whilst addressing difficulties.
- Focus on the impact of the circumstances of the child.
- Look at the whole picture – not only what has happened to the child, but the child's health and development, and the wider family and environmental context.
- Make full use of existing sources of information.
- Use a range of resources and techniques in communicating and working with children and families.

(Convention on the Rights of the Child, adopted and opened for signature, ratification and accession by General Assembly Resolution 44/25, 20 November 1989)

The key principles underpinning the UNCRC, your own guidelines and professional codes are at the heart of good practice. They highlight the responsibilities that each worker has in safeguarding and promoting the welfare of children. They should form the backdrop to practice, even when struggling with the many pressures and demands of day-to-day work and scarcity of resources. Translating these principles to the professional context for practice in child neglect means that:

- responsibility must be practised in a multi-agency context;
- all child care workers and helping agencies have a responsibility to safeguard and protect children and promote their well-being;
- each agency will have different contributions to make towards safeguarding and promoting the welfare of children, depending on the functions for which they have responsibility;
- neglect is less likely to be recognised by a single professional working in isolation from other professionals;
- multi-agency discussion and information-sharing is crucial to both the identification and management of cases; and
- working in isolation, within or between agencies, can lead to unsafe decisions.

Understand the legislative, regulatory and practice guidance framework

Each agency will have access to the legislative and regulatory framework for this area of work, and will mediate this through its own practice guidance. The key legislation for practitioners in the different countries of the UK is set out below. Newly appointed practitioners should become familiar with relevant legislation, regulations and practice guidance through induction training and good supervision provided by their agency or local children's safeguarding board. The remit of this book does not allow for a detailed outline of these, so you should ensure that you have read the relevant documents and/or can easily access them for reference, as well as having access to your own organisation's policies and procedures. The legislative and practice framework, professional values and ethics form the basic framework for practice in the area of safeguarding.

Legislation – England and Wales

- Children Act 1989
- Children Act 2004
- Safeguarding Vulnerable Groups Act 2006
- Children Act 2008

Legislation – Scotland

- Children (Scotland) Act 1995
- Protection of Children and Prevention of Sexual Offences (Scotland) Act 2005
- Protection of Vulnerable Groups (Scotland) Act 2007
- Children's Hearings (Scotland) Act 2011 (from 2012)

Legislation – Northern Ireland

- Children Order 1995
- The Safeguarding Vulnerable Groups (Northern Ireland) Order 2007 and Safeguarding Vulnerable Groups (Regulated Activity, Devolution Alignment and Miscellaneous Provisions) Order (Northern Ireland) 2010

Guidance – England

- *Working Together to Safeguard Children* (2010)
- *Framework for the Assessment of Children in Need and their Families* (2000)
- *What to do if you are Worried a Child is being Abused* (2003)
- Common Assessment Framework (2005)

Guidance – Wales

- *Working Together* (2004)
- *All Wales Child Protection Procedures* (2002)
- *Framework for the Assessment of Children in Need and their Families* (2002)
- Children Act 2004 section 28

Guidance – Scotland

- *National Guidance for Child Protection in Scotland* (2010)
- *National Guidance – Under-age Sexual Activity: Meeting the needs of children and young people and identifying child protection concerns* (2010)
- *The Role of the Registered Social Worker in Statutory Interventions: Guidance for local authorities* (2010)
- *A Guide to Getting it Right for Every Child* (2008)

Guidance – Northern Ireland
- Children (NI) Order 1995 Regulations and Guidance, Vol 6: *Co-operating to protect children*
- *Co-operating to Safeguard Children* (2003)
- *Understanding the Needs of Children in Northern Ireland* (2007)

Consider the culture of your work environment

A safe and favourable work environment is one that, in addition to having clear organisational expectations, procedures, and delineation of roles and responsibilities, is a supportive, listening and learning one. It ensures that individual workers have realistic workloads, the tools to do their work, including opportunities for training and development, and good working conditions. Lapses in safeguarding are more likely if workers have unrealistically high caseloads or if teams are not staffed appropriately and a backlog of work builds up. The safety and welfare of workers should be a priority, taking into account the hostility and aggression from family members that workers may encounter. You should have access to good supervision in the context of an organisational environment that encourages a 'culture of enquiry' (Parrott *et al*, 2007). In other words, you should be encouraged to question, to think outside the box, to challenge, to explore different ways of thinking and working. This is particularly important in the area of child neglect where there is confusion about thresholds for intervention.

Safeguarding practice should be at the heart of every level of the organisation, with a strong commitment to multi-agency working and to ensuring that the child is always at the centre of your work.

> *When a newly qualified social worker joins the team and is horrified by what they see in some families and asks why we didn't take the child into care, it makes you sit up and think. Have I just got used to this? Is this what I now expect? It makes you ask yourself whether you shouldn't have done more. I know they're new and enthusiastic and sometimes a bit naive but it makes you think...*
>
> *(Experienced children's social worker)*

Beliefs and practice will be shaped by individual values and experiences, different personal interpretations of the meaning of "good enough" parenting and of thresholds for intervention. At the team level, your manager may be very influential in determining practice. The community within which you work, your relationships with colleagues in other disciplines and the resources available to you will also influence practice. You may be working in a community where there is a culture of non-co-operation with public authorities. If your role involves seeing neglect on a daily basis, there is a real risk of becoming desensitised to children's experiences. Your responses may be different from those of the neighbouring team that rarely sees a neglect case: in other words, your own threshold can be raised. Good supervision which encourages reflective practice should help you to maintain personal vigilance.

In this challenging area of work, you are inevitably working with unpredictability, uncertainty and anxiety (Ruch, 2007). The response of organisations to this has been what Ruch calls 'technical-rational', leading to bureaucratic and risk-averse approaches to practice. This perspective may be a way of managing the complexity of the situations you work with, but it won't necessarily help you understand nor be creative. A way of working based on reflective practice, on the other hand, acknowledges the uniqueness of every situation and the individuals involved, the complexity of the work, and allows for the use of different forms of knowledge and understanding to be applied.

To become effective reflective practitioners, you need what Bion (1962) calls a 'containing' environment, one that allows workers to explore their feelings, their uncertainties and their fear of 'not knowing'. Reflective practice encourages the use of theory, knowledge and experience in developing different ways of understanding the situations you work with. It provides you with an opportunity to analyse and evaluate your work. It helps you consider what you know about families and how you have come to know this. It helps to develop understanding and critical thinking skills so that you can apply new learning to your practice. Reflective practice helps you challenge your usual ways of thinking, makes you ask yourself whether there isn't some other way of understanding what you see before you. It means that you act and plan on the basis of your reflections so that your practice remains relevant, creative and attuned to need.

You may want to consider what opportunities you have for reflective practice in your work environment. Ideally, supervision should promote this, providing you with a space to explore your thinking and feeling and to make sense of the complexities of your caseload. Peer group supervision and team case discussions can provide other useful forums.

> *This requires from colleagues what Ruch (2007) calls 'emotional listening', where the emphasis is on encouraging reflection on the 'being' experiential aspects of involvement as well as the 'doing'. The aim should be to allow and embrace expression of the complexity of practice and the relationships and feelings involved, halting the search for simple 'doing' solutions (such as more procedures) which leave the emotional, relational components out and prevent true understanding of the worker's experience, the child's life and what needs to be done.*
>
> (Ferguson, 2009, pp 477–78)

Consider also the opportunities you have to reflect on your work with colleagues in other disciplines.

Consider your awareness of issues of diversity and difference

When working with children and families, consider the impact you personally have on those you are trying to engage with. Issues of ethnicity, culture, class, gender, age and sexuality are all factors, in addition to your professional role, that will have a bearing on your relationship with families. You need to consider any barriers these factors raise and the impact they might have on the response you receive and the assessment you make.

If you are a white practitioner working with a family from a black or minority ethnic background, how are you likely to be seen? What is your understanding about this family's culture, religious practices and parenting practices? Remember that one of the big mistakes made in the case of Victoria Climbié was the false, and racist, assumption about her relationship with her great-aunt. On the other hand, although there is a higher proportion of black and minority ethnic children in the UK with child protection plans, this does not mean that more black and minority ethnic parents maltreat their children or that they are more likely to have punitive attitudes towards parenting. For many of these families, being black is also associated with a high incidence of poverty, poor housing and unemployment and oppressive practice.

Being sensitive to cultural and class differences is important, but you need to beware of allowing fear of imposing your own values to obscure the signs of neglect. Other differences may affect your responses. A young female worker who feels intimidated by a physically powerful and hostile father may unconsciously avoid meeting him and as a result fail to register the significance of his presence in the home. We know that disabled children are more vulnerable to maltreatment than non-disabled children. The lack of awareness of the impact of having a disabled child in the family, the application of a model of understanding disability that focuses only on the impairment, or not having the means of communicating with a disabled child may all result in missing signs of maltreatment.

Consider your sensitivity to issues of difference and diversity. If you are aware that you lack knowledge in certain areas, do you know where you can access information, guidance or consultation? You might find it helpful to carry out what McCracken (quoted in Holland, 2004) calls a 'cultural review'. This involves asking yourself a series of questions, such as those given below.

- What do I know about families like this one, and how do I know what I know (difference might be to do with ethnicity, class, disability, different social groups in society)?
- What beliefs/values/prejudices do I have and where do these come from?
- What am I expecting from this family and what might surprise me?
- How am I likely to be perceived by this family, and what do they understand or think about the agency I represent?

Where you may be working with families whose first language is not English, ensure that you are able to address any language barriers, and work with an interpreter where necessary, making sure that they understand the purpose of your involvement and the focus of your interview. Child development is similar across cultures and the same factors can cause delay and distress. Find out about the family's cultural background; test out your thinking with colleagues and your supervisor, seeking help from a consultant with expert knowledge where appropriate. Be aware of the different forms of support available to a family, for example, religious and community leaders. Ensure that you explain carefully what intervention you are planning and the anticipated outcomes. As with all families, check and re-check your understanding and judgements as new information comes to light.

Consider the barriers to effective working in the arena of neglect

There are a number of common themes that permeate serious case reviews that are undertaken when a child has died or been subject to serious injury. Consider how these themes could inform your own practice and that of your organisation.

Desensitisation and accommodation

The conclusions of serious case reviews appear to show that the more you come into contact with families where neglect is an issue, the greater the risk of becoming desensitised to neglect and its impact on children's lives. There is a risk that you could see this family as "no different from all the other families on this estate" – you accommodate to their standards of poor parenting. Or, because the parents co-operate when you ask them to do something, you take this as a positive sign that overrides all the negatives.

"Start again" syndrome

Working with neglect can feel overwhelming and disempowering for practitioners, and one way of managing this is to set aside what has happened in the past and focus only on the present – to start again. You may feel that you have done all you can with a family and decide to refer them on to another agency, with the hope that the new one will be able to make a fresh start with a new approach and a new relationship with the family. This can result in discontinuity for the family, who may already have difficulty in engaging with services and may not trust anyone to make a difference. It can also result in critical information, or the insight of particular workers, being lost. The story may be new to each worker but the experience of ongoing neglect in the past and present continues to erode the child's development.

Fear

Anger and hostility from parents are emotions that workers may face on a regular basis. If mechanisms to protect you are not in place, efforts to engage parents or to challenge their behaviour can be jeopardised by anxiety about your own safety. You may then feel unable to address your concerns about the children. Fear of attack – verbal or physical – may change your perception of what is going on in the family. You need a safe place, for example, in supervision, in which to address how some parents might make you feel and the ways in which these feelings may affect your vision and practice. You need to ask yourself: 'If I feel frightened when I go into this home, what are the children likely to feel?'

Culture of optimism

> **Rule of optimism:**
> **A dimension of the organisational culture of child protection services which is founded on the deep ambivalence that we feel in a liberal society about state intervention in families.**
>
> (Dingwall et al, 1995, p 247)

One of the principal aims of intervention is to empower service users and to give them the skills and knowledge to take control of their own lives. Assessments aim to identify strengths as well as weaknesses, and to build on those strengths. You want to keep children within their families wherever possible; you want parents to succeed in looking after their children. However, if you only focus on the positives, there is a risk of losing sight of the child who may be insidiously harmed. Parental efforts to change and small signs of improvement can sometimes lull workers into a false sense of optimism. You may work with a parent who knows exactly how much they need to do to make you satisfied that things are changing for the better, when actually no real change is taking place.

Focus on the parent, not the child

One of the criticisms that appear in serious case reviews is that of the focus of work being on the parent rather than the child. There is a particular risk of this happening in cases of neglect. Many neglecting parents are themselves very needy individuals who live chaotic and disorganised lives. They may often feel helpless in the face of their many problems and lack control over their lives. It is not surprising, therefore, that empathy for the adults can mean that the focus on the child gets lost.

Thresholds

The lack of clarity or common agreement about thresholds for neglect is an issue that applies not only to individual practitioners but also across the disciplines working with children and families. It is not uncommon for colleagues from health, education and children's social services to have very different ideas about what constitutes neglect and what operates as a threshold for intervention. This difference can stem from personal views and experience, professional perspectives and availability of resources.

Misinterpreting the signs of neglect

All the barriers to intervention discussed above can contribute to the misinterpretation of signs of neglect. But misinterpreting can also be about a lack of sound knowledge of different theoretical perspectives; not seeing or listening to children; misattributing behaviour to a child's disability; a lack of working together with other services involved with the family; or mistaken cultural assumptions.

Consider how confident and competent you feel in working with neglect cases

Having read this first chapter on the context of working with child neglect, you might like to consider the following questions.

- How competent and confident do you feel about working with neglect cases?
- What helps? What would help increase your sense of competence and confidence?
- How well does your employing organisation support you in working with neglect cases?
- Do you have any particular training and development needs that would improve your practice and confidence? Do you have access to current literature and research on child neglect?
- Do you have sufficient opportunity for reflection, in supervision and as a team?
- Do your professional relationships with other services promote working together?
- Is the welfare of the child always at the centre of what you do?
- What can you do to ensure good practice in working with child neglect?

TIP 2

Learn the lessons from serious case reviews

Serious case reviews are held when a child dies (including by suicide) and abuse or neglect are known or suspected to be a factor in the death. A review may also be undertaken when a child has sustained a life-threatening or serious injury and permanent impairment of health or development has resulted from abuse or neglect. Only a minority of children who suffer serious injury through abuse or neglect will be subject to serious case review. The main aim of holding such a review is to learn the lessons and to support improvements in services locally. However, these reports often provide valuable lessons for all professionals working in safeguarding services.

Overview reports (Brandon *et al*, 2008, 2009; Rose and Barnes, 2008) that consider and analyse the findings from serious case reviews are useful reading, as they highlight common themes and identify important lessons for practice. It is, however, dispiriting to see that the themes and lessons of these reports are ones that have been repeated since the first major review in 1974 was undertaken, following the death of Maria Colwell. Two other important publications which analyse child deaths are those by Reder *et al* (1993), titled *Beyond Blame: Child abuse tragedies revisited*, and Reder and Duncan (1999), titled *Lost Innocents: A follow-up study of fatal child abuse.*

One of the purposes of undertaking serious case reviews is to get beyond the blame and criticism that often results when a child suffers a serious injury or dies, and to try and make sense of the events and the behaviour of the people involved. This can be a painful and emotive process as the history of involvement of different agencies with the family, their interventions and responses are scrutinised.

Be aware of the prevalence of child neglect in those cases subject to serious case reviews

The most common category under which children are subject to child protection plans is neglect (44.4 per cent at year ending March 2010 in England) (DfE, 2010b). Neglect is a recurring theme in serious case reviews; although it is often an incident of physical or sexual abuse that causes the serious injury or death of a child, in many cases chronic neglect has been a feature. Sidebotham (2007) concludes that up to 40 per cent of maltreatment-related deaths are probably the result of either neglect or a combination of neglect and other forms of abuse. Neglect cases have included overlying (a parent lying on an infant in bed), illness, accidents, house fires and other indications of neglect and emotional abuse (Brandon *et al*, 2008). Neglect is often associated with domestic violence, mental health difficulties and substance misuse in parents' lives, which can create a 'toxic' environment for the child (Brandon *et al*, 2009). It is not unusual to see a pattern of neglect from one generation to the next. It is a worrying feature that, in many cases, children have been neglected over a prolonged period with varying levels of intervention by different agencies, but with no significant action being taken until a particular incident triggers protective action. There can be a "neglect of neglect" by agencies, with other concerns having higher priority.

The majority of serious case reviews have been undertaken in respect of children under the age of two years (47 per cent under two in the years 2001–2003; 47 per cent and 45 per cent under the age of 12 months in years 2003–05 and 2005–07 respectively). However, there have also been a worrying number of reviews relating to young people who have been seriously injured through self-harm, attempted or actual suicide. Brandon *et al* (2008) refer to these young people as 'hard to help' – young people with histories of severe maltreatment and rejection, missing school, having had numerous placement breakdowns, going missing, and having long-term involvement with a number of agencies. Brandon and colleagues write of 'agency neglect' in relation to these young people, where agencies have either not responded to their needs or not responded in a sustained and productive manner.

Consider some of the main themes emerging from serious case reviews

Loss of focus on the child, focus on the adults

Neglect cases are complex and difficult to work with. There is never a single cause of chronic neglect but rather a multiplicity of factors, which often include social and economic deprivation and parents with a range of psychological, social and mental health difficulties. In some cases attention has been diverted, because of the disorganised and chaotic lives of the family, from the child to the adult. Practitioners have been "hijacked" by the adults, sometimes owing to the pressing nature of their needs but also, in some cases, as a deliberate attempt by the parents to deflect interest away from the children. At the same time, some workers have not persevered hard enough to ensure that they see the child and have accepted parents' explanations for their absence. Decisions have been made without the voice of the child being heard and intervention has been geared to addressing the adult difficulties rather than focusing on the lived experience of the child. Victoria Climbié was such a child: she was never asked for her story and subsequently dangerous, and ultimately fatal, assumptions were made (House of Commons Health Committee, 2003). Given the high proportion of very young children subject to serious case reviews –

children who do not have a voice – it is imperative that the child is always at the centre of your attention.

Lack of overview or reflection on events

Neglect is rarely the result of a single incident but is likely to occur over a period of time, with some children experiencing neglect over a number of years. Within this period, several referrals may have been made to children's social care services and been dealt with as one-off referrals by duty teams, or may have been cases that were opened and closed a number of times with different practitioners involved. Practice in neglect cases tends to be reactive rather than proactive. You will find it difficult to capture the true nature of what is happening to a child unless you, and the other professional services involved, take an overview of the case. You need a perspective that encompasses the views of different professionals and takes into account the history of referrals and intervention. Where this overview has been missing, referrals or incidents have been seen in isolation and the true picture has not emerged until a serious incident occurs and a full chronology is undertaken. This has sometimes been the first opportunity for a proper analysis and reflection on events.

Poor assessment and analysis

Incomplete or poor assessments lacking in risk assessment and analysis are mentioned in many of the serious case review reports. Initial optimism about parenting capacity can become the dominant view, even in the light of later conflicting evidence. This is particularly risky until there is a serious event that changes people's perceptions. Risks can also remain unseen if the balance of the assessment is tipped to an over-emphasis on identifying positives. Everyone wants families to succeed in caring for their children, and there is always a risk of this leading to a 'rule of optimism' (Laming, 2003) which then distorts the real picture.

Overview reports identify assessments as sometimes being too static and linear, without a proper appreciation of the interaction between the three domains of the assessment framework. Insufficient weight is given to the parents' histories and the impact of their mental health difficulties, domestic violence and substance misuse on the child's development and well-being. Workers sometimes engage in fixed thinking, i.e. identifying a case as one of neglect and failing to see signs of physical injury.

Key messages for social workers undertaking assessments

- Focus on the child's well-being.
- Know who is in the family.
- Get a social and family history.
- Use genograms and chronologies.
- Ensure that the child/children are seen and heard.
- Focus on the child's attachments.
- Gather and analyse information within an ecological framework.
- Understand the dynamic nature of child development interacting with the other domains of the assessment framework.
- Address the risk of harm in the context of evidence about risk factors.
- Pay attention to injuries to the child.
- Notice and question anxious help-seeking of parents.
- Differentiate between material and emotional neglect.
- If a child is developmentally delayed, ask yourself whether he or she is being neglected.
- Distinguish between active and passive co-operation from parents.
- Discuss evidence and emerging thinking with professional colleagues from your own and other services involved with the family.
- Analyse the information gathered within an ecological framework.

(Compilation of messages from analyses of serious case reviews, Brandon et al, 2008, 2009; Rose and Barnes, 2008)

Not recognising indications of risk of harm from chronic neglect

We know that the long-term impact of neglect on the health and development of children can be far more serious than the effects of physical harm and even of sexual abuse. Those neglect cases that 'bump along the bottom' (Brandon *et al*, 2009) will include children whose early brain development has been significantly compromised by poor care and lack of stimulation. Only responding to an incident of abuse or an accident can mean ignoring a pattern of chronic neglect, the signs of which may include developmental delay, poor school attendance, frequent minor injuries and illnesses, failure to attend for health appointments, being dirty and smelly and living in unhygienic conditions. The failure to perceive or a misinterpretation of signs can result in either no action or inappropriate action. The language we use to describe children's experiences is also significant. Brandon and colleagues (2008) discuss the use of the term "rough handling" and how this terminology may mask what is actually physical abuse. The anti-social behaviour that labels children as "naughty boys" may disguise children in need. The attitudes and values we have also affect our response. For example, signs of maltreatment that would have merited a child protection plan in a non-disabled child have met with a less than rigorous approach for disabled children (Rose and Barnes, 2008).

Not acting on assessment or loss of momentum

Incomplete or poor assessments may result in unsafe decision-making and lack of action. Signs of neglect may be considered insufficiently serious for action. Workers may find it difficult to keep track of families who are always on the move and may be deliberately avoiding professional intervention. Cases of chronic neglect need long-term multi-agency intervention, which is difficult to sustain in the face of parental resistance and anger, and their sense of hopelessness and helplessness. The chaos, confusion and feelings of hopelessness in the parents can transmit to the professionals around them, and become reflected in confused, half-hearted interventions by workers. Where your intervention fails to result in change, you may wish to close the case or refer it to another agency; or you may see the lack of engagement by parents as a reason to close a case. The risk is that the children involved continue to "bump along the bottom" until a serious incident occurs; meanwhile, their well-being is eroded.

Over-optimism about parental capacity in difficult circumstances

Parents (often, although not solely, mothers) can appear to manage in the most difficult of circumstances, when in fact this is far from the case. Starting from the principle that it is better for children to be brought up by their parents, inevitably we want to see them succeed. In many situations, parents, and their children, are actually clinging on desperately to survive, living in conditions of deprivation with multiple difficulties, including those resulting from their own impoverished upbringings. This struggle against the odds may continue until either a serious incident or the accumulating pressure of problems can tip families over the edge. Some parents have several children and instead of being more concerned about their ability to cope with another one, the risk is that we assume that their experience of parenting previous children will carry them through (Brandon *et al*, 2008). This focus on the desire for families to succeed, coupled with the lack of a major incident of maltreatment, can sometimes prevent workers from noticing the signs of poor or inadequate parenting, and lead to an assumption that the children will be all right.

Poor information sharing, recording, management, supervision and training

In most cases, making sense of signs and symptoms of neglect relies on the pooling of information from different services. To gain a true picture of chronic neglect requires comprehensive chronologies (and a sound understanding of child development patterns), thorough case recording and management oversight to enable patterns of behaviour and parenting to be identified over time. A mutual understanding of the signs of neglect and agreement about thresholds for intervention develops from talking to your colleagues in other services. Where there is a divergence of views about thresholds and intervention, this can result in professional paralysis and, ultimately, the toleration of poor parenting (Rose and Barnes, 2008). Effective working together depends on relationships based on mutual trust and respect and a willingness to debate the issues. The key roles of other organisations, such as education, health, the police, youth services, CAMHS, and housing should not be underestimated. Multi-agency training can help to break down some of the barriers to understanding professional perspectives, but don't forget that the best way to communicate is face to face. Good supervision and opportunities for reflection and support can aid working together.

Understand factors common to children who die or suffer serious injury from neglect

Neglect features in many serious case reviews. From the intensive sample of 47 children in one overview report (Brandon *et al*, 2008), 15 were identified as neglect cases, six of whom were under the age of one year and often the last in a series of pregnancies, not all resulting in live births. Most of the young children had difficulties at birth and mothers' attendance for health appointments was poor. These children received inappropriate physical care and/or abuse and were often left with inappropriate carers. These factors highlight the importance of the role of midwives and health visitors in identifying early risk signs.

The older group of teenagers in the study, deemed difficult to help (15 of the intensive sample of 47), had experienced a history of rejection, loss and maltreatment which included neglect over lengthy periods of time. These may have been some of the young children with signs of chronic neglect that were either ignored or misinterpreted by the multiple agencies involved. As young people, they were involved in self-harm and substance misuse.

Only a minority of the children subject to serious case reviews had child protection plans, but all were in receipt of universal services and some were identified as children in need. This underlines the fact that safeguarding is everybody's business.

Be able to identify features common to neglectful parents

Emotional and physical neglect and sexual exploitation are common to the histories of parents who maltreat their children. Parents have often spent time in public care or in the care of relatives, have experienced frequent house moves and left home at an early age. The absence of father figures, the lack of information about the biological father, a succession of adult male figures in the child's life and little information about maternal grandfathers are common factors. Criminality and violence also feature in the lives of fathers. Mothers have often had multiple pregnancies, some ending in miscarriage, termination or loss of the child through adoption or being cared for by a relative. Mental health difficulties are common amongst mothers involved in neglect cases, as are alcohol and drug misuse in both parents. Attitudes of ambivalence, resistance and hostility towards helping agencies are common. These are not causal factors, but you should recognise them as increasing the risk of harm to a child and take note of them in your assessment. Such factors support the need for holistic assessments that include a complete social and family history, and the need to work closely with adult services. They also highlight the challenge of working with parents who are hostile and ambivalent towards professional services.

Reflect on how you and your agency respond to working with neglectful parents and their children

Although some parents will try to avoid the involvement of professional services, the response families receive from these services merits examination. From the parents' perspective, it can sometimes feel as though they are being avoided and rebuffed (Brandon *et al*, 2008). This has taken the form of agencies offering a succession of different workers, opening and closing cases, referring cases on, or initiating then halting care proceedings. For families who already live chaotic and disorganised lives, these responses can only appear confusing. They may reflect the emotional impact on practitioners of working with neglect, as well as confusion and disagreement about signs, thresholds and other barriers mentioned earlier.

Some of the children suffering neglect are not known to children's social care but are in receipt of universal services or family support services. Practitioners delivering these services can be the least qualified or experienced of the children's workforce. They are, therefore, at a disadvantage in dealing with some of the most complex cases that require a greater depth of knowledge, skill and expertise in order to recognise when a situation should be referred for targeted or statutory services. In some of the cases leading to serious case review, it was clear that children should have been identified as children in need and had a core assessment long before the incident that triggered action at a higher level (Rose and Barnes, 2008).

How well do you share information with other agencies? Are you clear about confidentiality?

Six-year-old Sam's attendance at school is poor. He attends in unsuitable clothing and falls asleep in class. The family's health visitor is concerned that the new baby in the family is failing to put on weight and that his mother has missed appointments at the clinic. The house is dirty and cold and there is little food. Someone has smelt drink on the mother's breath when she is out with the children. The housing department has had complaints from neighbours about noise at night and the mess in the garden. Children's services has had intermittent contact with the family over the years. The picture of neglect depends on people pooling this information and interpreting it in relation to the lived experiences of the children in that household. Where you think a child may be at risk of harm, you should share information. If in any doubt, consult your manager, and *What to do if you're Worried a Child is being Abused* (DfES, 2006).

Key points

- Be aware of the risk factors associated with neglect (remember that risk factors do not *predict* neglect).
- Health professionals, particularly midwives and health visitors, and those working in early years services have a key role to play in the early identification of neglect in babies and young children.
- Develop a common understanding within your service and those you work with of thresholds for identifying neglect.
- Ensure that your assessment is evidence-based and analytical, and focuses on the impact of that evidence on the child's health and development.
- Forge relationships with colleagues in other services working with the family. Effective working together is easier to achieve where professionals have created a relationship based on trust and respect.

TIP 3

Recognise when a child is being neglected

Think of a child who is dear to you, and make a list of all the things you would want for this child. You are likely to come up with many suggestions which might include 'to feel safe and secure', 'to be loved', 'to have a warm home', 'to be well fed and clothed', 'to be able to play and have fun', 'to go to school', 'to be given opportunities to fulfil their potential', and so on.

Isn't this what you want for all children, not just those whom you know and love? If a child lacks one or more of the things you have suggested, does this constitute child neglect? The answer is complicated. Neglect and its impact will depend on the age of the child, the relationship they have with their caregivers, whether it is a one-off omission or commission or something which persists over time alongside other unmet needs. Most parents will admit to a lapse of care or an inadequate response to a child's needs once in a while. But the difference is in the attitude towards and meaning of being a parent and the enduring relationship with the child.

This chapter considers what we mean by the term "neglect", its nature and signs. Many local authorities have their own protocols for working with child neglect and there is useful guidance from NICE (2009) for medical practitioners and others in health services.

Understand what children need for healthy development

When the *Every Child Matters* agenda was introduced in England and Wales in 2003, its aim was to improve outcomes for all children and young people. The five outcome areas remain relevant today.

The *Every Child Matters* five outcomes are:
- Be healthy
- Be safe
- Enjoy and achieve
- Make a positive contribution
- Achieve economic well-being

   (DCSF, 2003)

Similar initiatives have also been undertaken in Scotland (*Getting it Right for Every Child*) and Northern Ireland (*Our Children and Young People: Our pledge*).

Cooper (1985) identified a set of basic needs, which remains current today (see below). You may wish to use this framework when thinking of the lives of children you know. Consider what it means to a child if one of these areas of need is unmet.

- ***Basic physical care:*** *which includes warmth, shelter, adequate food and rest, grooming (hygiene) and protection from danger.*
- ***Affection:*** *which includes physical contact, holding, stroking, cuddling and kissing, comforting, admiration, delight, tenderness, patience, time, making allowances for annoying behaviour, general companionship and approval.*
- ***Security:*** *which involves continuity of care, the expectation of continuing in the stable family unit, a predictable environment,*

consistent patterns of care and daily routine, simple rules and consistent controls and a harmonious family group.

- **Stimulation and innate potential:** *by praise, by encouraging curiosity and exploratory behaviour, by developing skills through responsiveness to questions and to play, by promoting educational opportunities.*

- **Guidance and control:** *to teach adequate social behaviour which includes discipline within the child's understanding and capacity and which requires patience and a model for the child to copy, for example, in honesty and concern and kindness for others.*

- **Responsibility:** *for small things at first such as self-care, tidying playthings, or taking dishes to the kitchen, and gradually elaborating the decision-making that the child has to learn in order to function adequately, gaining experience through his/her mistakes as well as his/her successes, and receiving praise and encouragement to strive and do better.*

- **Independence:** *to make his/her own decisions, first about small things but increasingly about the various aspects of his/ her life within the confines of the family and society's codes. Parents use fine judgement in encouraging independence, and in letting the child see and feel the outcome of his/her capacity. Protection is needed, but over-protection is as bad as too early responsibility and independence.*

(Cooper, 1985, p 31)

Understand what we mean by the term "neglect"

Neglect is not easy to define. Unlike physical or sexual abuse where the definition is centred on an act of abuse, definitions of neglect often focus on omission rather than commission. It is difficult to "see" neglect and the experience of neglect depends on timing (Perry, 2002). For example, infants need touch for survival, teenagers don't. Perry defines neglect as 'the absence of critical organising experiences at key times during development' (p 88). A simple definition might be that a child's needs are not met (Jowitt, 2003). A narrow interpretation of neglect might focus only on physical neglect to the exclusion of emotional neglect. Interpretation may be affected by parental intention and practitioners' understanding of children's needs. Neglect could be a one-off incident, or episodes of neglect or chronic neglect.

> *It's so difficult, isn't it? It depends on the situation. You can't say that every parent who forgets to send their child to school with the right sports equipment or money or whatever is neglecting them. I know I've done it. But I know sometimes it is neglect.*
>
> *(Social work assistant)*

The definition of neglect that may be most familiar to workers in England and Wales is that in *Working Together to Safeguard Children* (DCSF, 2010).

> *Neglect is the persistent failure to meet a child's basic physical and/or psychological needs, likely to result in the serious impairment of the child's health or development. Neglect may occur during pregnancy as a result of maternal substance abuse. Once a child is born, neglect may involve a parent or carer failing to:*
>
> - *provide adequate food, clothing and shelter (including exclusion from home or abandonment);*
> - *protect a child from physical and emotional harm or danger;*
> - *ensure adequate supervision (including the use of inadequate care-givers); or*
> - *ensure access to appropriate medical care or treatment.*
>
> *It may also include neglect of, or unresponsiveness to, a child's basic emotional needs.*
>
> *(DCSF, 2010)*

'Persistent' and 'serious' are key terms here; 'psychological' includes cognitive and emotional development (Stevenson, 2007). Neglect often goes side by side with emotional abuse:

Emotional abuse is the persistent emotional maltreatment of a child such as to cause severe and persistent adverse effects on the child's emotional development. It may involve conveying to children that they are worthless or unloved, inadequate, or valued only insofar as they meet the needs of another person. It may include not giving the child opportunities to express their views, deliberately silencing them or 'making fun' of what they say or how they communicate. It may feature age or developmentally inappropriate expectations being imposed on children. These may include interactions that are beyond the child's developmental capability, as well as overprotection and limitation of exploration and learning, or preventing the child participating in normal social interaction. It may involve seeing or hearing the ill-treatment of another. It may involve serious bullying (including cyberbullying), causing children frequently to feel frightened or in danger, or the exploitation or corruption of children. Some level of emotional abuse is involved in all types of maltreatment of a child, though it may occur alone.

(DCSF, 2010)

Neglect can occur before birth and can be particularly pernicious for young children. It affects their capacity to form secure attachments, their health and development and can have serious long-term effects on social functioning, educational achievement and relationships. Neglect and emotional abuse are often closely linked. Cases of neglect and emotional abuse are characterised by the nature of the environment the child lives in rather than existing as an identifiable 'event' (Glaser and Prior, 1997). The parent who neglects to change a nappy or feed an infant is not only neglecting physical needs but is also insensitive to the emotional needs that are satisfied by the relief of stress and the provision of comfort. Neglect can be a failure to meet physical needs, but this may also involve a failure to recognise and respond to emotional needs, and/or a failure to recognise risk and protect from danger. Neglect can be difficult to define because it is rarely a single event. Chronic neglect has been described as 'the breakdown or absence of a relationship of care' (Taylor and Daniel, 2005, p 292). These authors refer to the pervasive nature of emotional neglect, describing it as 'the very "air that they breathe"'. Emotional neglect denies the psychological existence of the child and can have a profound effect on self-esteem and identity.

Jan Horwath's definition of neglect is also useful.

> *Child neglect is a failure on the part of either the male and/or female caregiver or pregnant mother, to complete the parenting tasks required to ensure that the developmental needs of the child are met. This should take account of the age, gender, culture, religious beliefs and particular needs and circumstances of the individual child. This failure may be associated with parenting issues. It has occurred despite reasonable resources being available to enable the carer/s to complete the parenting tasks satisfactorily. Whilst neglect is likely to be ongoing, one-off incidents and episodic neglect can affect the health and development of a child.*
>
> *(2007, p 38)*

Consider the nature of neglect

We know that neglect can be difficult to define because it is multi-faceted. It is also the form of maltreatment most likely to be associated with low socio-economic status (Spencer and Baldwin, 2005). However, there is no simple association. You will know families living in poor circumstances, whose lives are stressful and difficult, who do not neglect their children (just as you may know families in comfortable circumstances, able to provide all sorts of opportunities for their children, who emotionally neglect them). This is not to say that we should ignore the impact of poverty nor stop working to eradicate it. But you need to consider what it is that differentiates those families who manage to meet the needs of their children with limited resources and under difficult circumstances from those who don't, those who care for their children from those who neglect them. In other words, you need to consider how poverty and environmental factors interact with parenting capacity. Factors that often come into play include a disorganised and chaotic lifestyle, lack of a good support system, lack of skills in managing scarce resources or resources being spent on drink and drugs instead of food, etc. In many cases, it is an inability or unwillingness to place the children's needs first. Ask yourself why there is no food in the fridge, or why the child goes to school inappropriately dressed. Is it because of financial difficulties? If so, what is the cause of this? Would financial help or support in managing finances improve matters?

Let us consider some of the different aspects of the *Working Together* definition of neglect (DCSF, 2010).

Pre-birth experiences

There is a wealth of research evidence on the effects on the development of the foetus of alcohol and drug use and smoking during pregnancy. Newborn babies may suffer drug withdrawal symptoms and there are a range of symptoms associated with Foetal Alcohol Effects (FAE) and Foetal Alcohol Spectrum Disorder (FASD). Our increasing knowledge about early brain development also means that we now have a more sophisticated understanding of the impact on the baby in the womb of high levels of maternal stress, for example, caused by domestic violence. The baby is vulnerable to the mother's lifestyle. Has the new mother responded to messages about health and lifestyle during pregnancy? Has she availed herself of ante-natal care? How motivated to change is she, and what help will she need to make these changes? Is the father present in her life? Does he acknowledge the risks and is he willing to support his partner and change his behaviour?

Basic needs

The domain of the child's developmental needs (DH, 2000a) and Cooper's list of basic needs (1985) are frameworks to help you identify whether or not a child's basic needs are being met. Such needs are universal and it is possible to evidence where they are not being met.

However, this doesn't prevent individual interpretation and the fear of cultural insensitivity influencing judgements.

There are different cultural practices in parenting. Some cultures, for example, will place greater value on education. But children's basic needs remain the same and, whilst it is important to give consideration and due regard to cultural practices, if a child's health and development are compromised in any way, you should be concerned. Consider the needs of the disabled child. Parenting children with certain impairments can be extremely difficult. Rather than accept a lower standard of care, think about what services might help the parent ensure the same positive outcomes for that child as others in the family. Young carers and unaccompanied asylum seekers have the same needs as other young people but these can sometimes be overlooked because of their particular situations.

Signs that basic needs may be unmet (sources of evidence in italics)

Infants
- Low birth weight; weight faltering *(centile charts, health and midwifery records)*
- Withdrawal from drugs at birth; at risk from blood-borne viruses *(health records)*
- Delay in physical development *(growth charts, health visitor records)*
- Lack of bonding and early attachment *(observation, midwifery and health visitor records)*
- Repetitive, self-soothing movements *(observation, reports from caregivers)*
- Physical signs such as bruises, burns from being left in dirty nappies too long, lesions that have become infected *(observation, health records)*

Pre-school and school age
- Delay in physical growth and development *(health, early years and education records)*
- Delay in cognitive, speech and language development *(health and education records)*

- Behavioural disturbance – excessive aggression, withdrawal, non-compliance, control *(observation, caregiver reports, reports from school)*
- Anxious, insecure attachments to primary caregivers *(observation, attachment checklists, caregiver reports, child reports)*
- Health problems, including hearing and sight difficulties *(school health)*
- Wetting and soiling *(school and health reports)*
- Poor hygiene, smelly and dirty *(observation, reports from school and others, including family members, neighbours)*
- Inappropriate and unsuitable clothing *(observation, reports from school and others)*
- Excessive appetite *(reports from caregivers, school and child; observation)*
- Self-harm *(reports from school, health, caregiver, child; observation)*
- Non-school attendance *(education records)*
- Attending school without proper equipment and clothing *(school reports)*
- Parents/carers do not attend school events *(school records)*
- Poor academic progress *(school reports)*
- Lack of evidence of toys *(observation and questioning)*
- Child not allowed to play outdoors *(child and caregiver reports)*
- Difficulty in forming and keeping relationships with peers *(observation, reports from caregivers, school, child and others)*

Adolescents
- Those signs above, plus:
- Anti-social behaviour *(reports from school, community, police)*
- Drug and alcohol use *(observation, reports from caregivers, school, police and others)*
- Being described as "beyond control" *(reports from caregivers, school and others)*
- Going missing, running away *(reports from school, police, caregivers, young person)*

The attachment relationship between the child and their primary caregiver can be the key to identifying neglect. The child with a secure attachment will feel loved, safe and secure, confident of having their needs met and competent to face the world. A sensitive and responsive parent or carer will be attuned to their child's needs and prioritise these. The neglected child is likely to have a difficult attachment relationship with their parent or carer which often indicates significant unmet needs. If the parent is unable to meet basic needs, the neglected child will feel unsafe, anxious and experience the stress related to unmet need. Observation of the child's behaviour and the way in which child and carer relate to each other can provide valuable information about the attachment relationship. See Fahlberg's attachment checklists (1994, pp 34–37).

One of the common coping mechanisms that neglected children use when they fail to get the required response from their caregivers is to withdraw. These children are often living in environments that are chaotic and disorganised, or depressed and lifeless, with adults who are needy themselves. These are the children who may go unseen and unrecognised; they will try to fade into the background. Rarely do neglected children shout to be heard. They rely on you to recognise them and respond to them.

Protecting from physical and emotional harm or danger

The conditions in the home can provide evidence of the extent to which basic needs are met and how the child is protected from physical danger and harm. Unhygienic conditions can be particularly dangerous to the health of infants and toddlers crawling on the floor. Dog food and dog mess left lying around are health hazards, as are alcohol, drugs or other dangerous substances within easy reach. Broken furniture in the home or left lying around in the garden can cause accidents and injury. Young children expected to get their own meals or left alone in the house are at risk of accidents. A home that is poorly maintained, where electric wires are bare or sockets overloaded, presents a fire risk. The local housing department may be able to provide evidence to support your own observations here.

Home conditions associated with neglect
- Dirty kitchen with unwashed dishes piling up.
- Dirty and sticky floors.

- Broken windows and garden full of old and unsafe furniture/machinery.
- Uncontrolled pets.
- Dog food and dog mess left lying around.
- Inadequate or poorly maintained light and heating.
- Lack of food in cupboards and fridge.
- House in general disrepair, physical hazards.
- Bedrooms lacking furniture, inadequate bedding.
- Dirty toilet/bathroom, lack of toiletries.
- Lack of evidence of toys.
- Medication/cleaning fluids left lying around.

As well as parents' alertness to physical danger, you need to consider their awareness of the child's personal safety needs. Who lives in the household? Who are frequent visitors to the home? What do you know about them and whether or not they constitute a risk to the child? What picture do you get when you add up all the minor accidents and injuries? These may or may not constitute physical abuse, but may signify a failure to protect and supervise.

Signs of emotional harm may be evident in the way a parent speaks to their child. Being told 'You are stupid', 'I wish I'd never had you' or 'You've ruined my life' are phrases that stick in a child's mind and can have a profound impact on their sense of identity and self-esteem. Constantly being put down makes a child feel worthless. High criticism and low warmth are common characteristics of verbal and non-verbal interchanges between neglectful and emotionally abusing parents and their children. Parents of neglected children also speak to them less often than parents of children who are not neglected.

Supervision

All children require adult guidance and supervision appropriate to their age. It not only provides boundaries and structure to their lives but provides them with a sense of security and safety. How often is the child left with different babysitters or unsuitable carers? What is the impact of being passed from one carer to another on the child's ability to form a secure attachment with their parent? Does the parent know where the young child is when playing outside the home? Are young children allowed to roam the streets without adult supervision? Are they expected to get themselves to school? Does the parent know, or show concern about, the whereabouts of their older children? Do they know what the children do when away from the home? Have the older children been in trouble with the police or other authorities?

Neglect of emotional needs

Children not only need a significant adult on whom they can rely for safety, comfort and the relief of stress or anxiety, but also someone who can acknowledge their individuality and uniqueness, accept them for who they are and offer encouragement and praise. In other words, children need a parent who is psychologically available to them and who values them. The parent who consistently fails to recognise the child's need for attention or who simply ignores the child is telling them that they do not matter. A lack of curiosity or interest in the child's world, whether it is how the child is feeling, the activity they are currently absorbed in or what is happening at school or with friends, sends a message to the child of worthlessness, lack of importance and invisibility.

> *Sometimes you just get the sense that they are going through the motions, do you know what I mean? They're beautifully turned out and very polite and well-behaved and everything, but there doesn't seem to be any love. You just want to give them a cuddle. You wonder what happens when you leave and they close the door...*
>
> (Social worker)

See the child, hear the child

The danger of the child being "lost" has already been mentioned. Although it sounds obvious, you cannot determine whether a child is being neglected or not unless you see and hear the child. You need to see where the child sleeps, plays and eats. Pre-verbal children will tell their story through their relationships, their health and general well-being. Developmental charts will tell part of the story. The general demeanour, alertness and responsiveness of an infant contribute to the story. Older children, given the right opportunity, support and encouragement, can often tell you what it is like to live at home. (See Tip 4 for more information on communicating with children.)

Recognise neglect in the disabled child

Research suggests that disabled children are much more likely to be neglected that non-disabled children, and yet few disabled children feature amongst those with child protection plans under the category of neglect. This raises a question about the extent to which agencies responsible for safeguarding are focused on the experiences of the disabled child. Do we think that disabled children don't experience neglect in the same way as non-disabled children (Kennedy and Wonnacott, 2005)? Disabled children are particularly vulnerable to neglect for a number of reasons: difficulty in communicating their needs; the number of different carers they may have through short breaks, residential school, etc; and signs of neglect being misattributed to their impairment. Having a disabled child can place a significant financial burden on families, but you need to look at the interaction of financial factors with others that operate in cases of neglect.

Kennedy and Wonnacott (2005) suggest that it is helpful to think in terms of "disabling barriers". To what extent do certain factors, such as the child's environment, service provision or lack of it, family circumstances and society's perception of disability, contribute to the neglect of the disabled child? You should beware of attributing the child's developmental delay to their impairment when it may, instead, signal neglect.

A focus on the parent–child relationship may give you a better understanding of the meaning of the child to the parent and how they view their caring role. Where the main focus of parenting the disabled child is on meeting basic physical needs, attention to emotional needs may be neglected. Think about how the child is experiencing their life; the strain of caring for the disabled child cannot be ignored but shouldn't be allowed to excuse poor parenting. Horwath (2002), cited in Kennedy and Wonnacott, reminds us that '"doing your best" is not the same as "good enough parenting"' (p 239).

Key points

- Understand a child's basic needs and what this means in terms of recognising neglect.
- Check your knowledge of child development and attachment.
- Seek evidence of neglect in the context of impact on the child's health and development.
- Remember that disabled children can be neglected.
- Talk to others.
- Ask yourself whether this would be good enough for a child dear to you.
- Consider the interaction of child factors, family and environmental factors and agency response.
- Understand the lived experience of the child or young person.

TIP 4

Listen to the child

> *My life started out in not a fair way. Our house was a tip. It was very cold – it had no heating and it had hardly anything in it. I was often hungry and remember vividly helping my little sister up on the counter to make ourselves a jam sandwich. I used to think, 'I have to grow up now and make myself something to eat because my mum is asleep and I am all alone in life.'*
>
> (Georgie, aged 11, quoted in Harris, 2008, p 8)

To really understand neglect and its impact on children, you need to get as close as you can to the child's lived experience. What does it feel like to be that five-week-old baby left in a cold, dark room in a dirty nappy, hungry and alone? What is it like physically and emotionally to be constantly in a highly stressed state? Think of the three-year-old child ignored, cold and without food, left to his own devices. Or the eight-year-old who wakes in the morning to find there are no clean clothes and no hot water to remove the smell of urine after wetting the bed; who has to go to school on his own without anything to eat after a night when he was kept up late by parents fighting or drinking. Or the twelve-year-old who has to look after younger siblings, ensure there is food for them at the same time as watching that their mother doesn't choke on her vomit as she lies comatose on the sofa.

This tip looks at how to ensure that you keep in touch with the child's experience and always hear the child's voice. In working with children, we should focus on developing meaningful relationships, creating time and space for communication and building, with the child, ways of communicating based on their own unique strengths and preferences (Helm, 2010, p 168). Not only is this critical to the assessment of the child's needs, their wishes and feelings; it can also be the foundation for building trusting relationships, enhancing self-esteem and self-awareness and building resilience (Helm, 2010). The attuned intervention of empathic professionals who make real efforts to understand the child's experience can be the beginning of developing trust and faith in adults for children whose "relationship of care" has broken down. So it is apparent that whilst intervention at a practical level is important to improve the quality of life of children who experience neglect, it is the relationship which will support healing and well-being.

The child has a right to be heard

Both UK legislation and the UNCRC put the child's welfare as the paramount consideration in decision-making about children. Social workers are required to ascertain the wishes and feelings of the child, to involve them in their care planning and decisions made about them. The UN Convention highlights the right of the child to be:

- treated with respect, honesty and care;
- listened to and have what they say taken seriously and acted on appropriately;
- consulted on their wishes and feelings where possible and practicable; and

● considered in relation to their needs arising from their racial and cultural heritage, language, religion, gender, sexuality, age and any disability.

We know, however, that the child's voice easily gets lost and they are not always involved in planning and decision-making. The failure of professionals to see things from the child's perspective has been highlighted in the findings of serious case reviews: children not being seen, not talked to or listened to, their behaviour unobserved (Brandon *et al*, 2008). They can easily get lost in the chaos and disorganisation of family life and adult needs. Neglected children are at greater risk of being unseen and forgotten as they are often "disengaged", having given up and turned inwards to try and meet their own needs.

When children have been consulted about what they want from their social workers, they indicate that they want people they can trust, who will listen to them, be available to them, be non-judgemental, offer non-directive support, have a sense of humour, be straight-talking and maintain confidentiality (Dalzell and Sawyer, 2007, p 56). The Scottish Executive has sought to emulate this in a Children's Charter.

Scotland's Children's Charter

Get to know us	Think carefully about how you use information about us
Speak to us	Put us in touch with the right people
Listen to us	Use your power to help
Take us seriously	Make things happen when they should
Involve us	Help us be safe
Respect our privacy	Think about our lives as a whole
Be responsible to us	

(Scottish Executive, 2004)

Be aware of the barriers to working with and listening to children, and consider how to overcome them

There can be a range of mechanisms at work preventing you from getting close to the child's experience. These may include:

- your personal values and beliefs about children and their right to be heard;
- the cultural and professional context in which you work;
- your motivation and skills in communicating with children and young people;
- the way in which neglected children present themselves;
- the difficulty for the neglected child in trusting professionals; and
- the capacity of the neglected child to tell their story, to express their wishes and feelings.

A reflexive approach to working with children, which involves thinking about your own position, feelings and beliefs, together with a real commitment to getting to know the child and understand their behaviour and how they communicate, is vital. Helping children and young people to open up to you will not be easy. It takes time, effort, good communication skills and the building of trusting relationships.

Working with children and young people is made more difficult when they have picked up negative views from parents about professionals, or been told not to talk to you. They may not be used to adults who are prepared to listen to them. They may be frightened and lack the skills to communicate their conflicted feelings. Some may be concerned about what happens to the information they give you.

Many practitioners have busy working lives and are expected to juggle many different demands. The culture within today's children's social care services, which focuses on targets and performance indicators, can mean that you spend more time in front of a computer than with children and their families. The opportunity to develop or practise skills in direct work can suffer as a result. Are you able to spend as much time as you need with children? Do you have enough time with them to get to know them properly and to build strong relationships? Alternatively, there may be some times when sitting in front of a computer can be a way to avoid the difficult, and often emotionally challenging, task of listening to the stories children have to tell you. If this does happen, you need to consider the reasons for this: if it is a lack of confidence and skills, you should explore avenues for further training; if it is the personal impact of the work, you may wish to seek an opportunity to discuss this in supervision.

Neglected children often present as passive and self-contained, uninvolved with the world and those around them. They can be undemanding, don't expect much of anyone and can slip into the background unnoticed. With poor attachment experiences, these children frequently have difficulty with social relationships and lack empathy. They are likely to have poor speech and language skills and difficulty in processing emotions. They are not easy children to work with and may elicit feelings of despair and helplessness in workers. It may be more tempting to visit the child with whom you know you can have a more satisfying exchange. It is important to be aware of how working with neglected children can make you feel, and not to mistake the powerful "mirroring" of the child's internal state with a feeling that you are useless to them.

If the child has mainly had experience of adults who are generally unavailable, unresponsive and unreliable, then they may not expect anything different from you. You may have an uphill struggle to engage their trust. Don't give up: the child will be aware of your interest. Repeated and consistent messages, turning up for meetings when you say you will, your undivided attention and a willingness to listen all tell the child that you are curious and concerned. Take the time to build a relationship of trust. Work at the child's pace. Your assessment will help you to understand the child's emotional and cognitive development.

Think about the child's attachment experiences and how these have affected the development of empathy, emotional regulation and the capacity to express feelings. Schofield (1998) shows that whereas the securely attached child is in touch with and able to express a range of feelings, the insecurely attached child will have learnt that it is better not to express how you feel, or may manage their feelings by splitting them into "good" and "bad". Consequently, the child with an avoidant attachment (a common attachment pattern in neglected children) may appear unaffected by events in their life. They are likely to be compliant and will tell you what they think you want to hear.

The ambivalently attached child may see you as the most special person in their life and appear to invite closeness whilst at the same time keeping their distance. The child with a disorganised pattern of attachment has not found a way of managing their emotions and may veer from anger to avoidance and withdrawal. It is important therefore, when ascertaining children's wishes and feelings, to rely on a range of sources of evidence. Use different tools for engaging the child; observe his behaviour with you, other adults and children. Talk to others who have contact with the child – much may be revealed in their drawings and writings at school. Listen to what others say about the child's communication and day-to-day functioning. Place the child's behaviour in the context of their history, relationships, development and overall functioning.

The child's story may be painful and distressing for both child and worker, and you may well want to protect the child from the further distress of having to repeat their story. But being able to tell their story to a trusted adult in a safe environment can help the child to process events; sharing the story can help them release some of the burden; active listening can give a powerful message about the availability of the worker.

McLeod (2008, p 106), quoted in Helm, provides some tips for making it easier for children and young people to express their views:

- *Stop, look and listen.*
- *Keep an open mind.*
- *Give the child some control.*
- *Start from where the child is.*
- *Give permission to talk.*
- *Avoid direct questions.*
- *Offer prompts and triggers.*
- *Provide information and explanations.*
- *Encourage questions.*
- *Check out understandings.*

(Helm, 2010, p 176)

Helm (2010) suggests that workers should undertake a cultural review in relation to working with each child. This should be a part of ongoing reflective practice, a process that should take place individually, with other members of the team and in supervision.

- *What do I know about children/young people of this age?*
- *Where does my knowledge come from?*
- *What biases or values may I hold (positive or negative)?*
- *What do I know about children's needs at this age?*
- *What might surprise me about this child/young person and why would this be a surprise?*
- *How might I be perceived by this child?*
- *What impact might my assessment have on their life; tonight, next month, next year?*
- *What norms do I take with me from my team and organisation (e.g. hierarchies of risk, resource implications, etc)?*

(Helm, 2010, pp 177–78)

Ensure that you have the necessary skills and confidence to work with children and young people

Hopefully, you will have access to training and support to help you develop skills in working with children and young people. You will also need access to regular supervision to help you manage the thoughts and feelings which this work can generate and to encourage reflective practice. You can use the following questions as a way of auditing your skills in building trust and encouraging self-worth.

Building trust

- **How good are you at showing respect for the child?**
  If a child sees that they are being treated with respect, then they will be able to see the relationship with you as a two-way process and thus invest their trust.
- **Can you show that you appreciate the child's situation?**
  This involves the child's life experiences, any delays in their development and, therefore, their ability to explore, learn and progress in their development.
- **Can you work at the child's pace?**
  This may mean being very patient, retracing or repeating areas of work, taking it slowly when discussing painful issues.

● **How good are you at watching and listening for signals?**
  You will need to pay close attention, as signals are not always overt. You should allow the child to fantasise and should be accepting of fantasies (don't brush them aside); they are often the child's way of getting a message across.

● **Can you allow the child to take the lead?**
  The child won't do this until they are ready, but when they take this step you should go along with it, and offer something back. The child should not be denied the opportunity to explore specific areas of their choice.

● **Can you help the child express their hopes and fears?**
  Exploring with the child where their fears lie, whom they feel able to trust, relating lack of trust to fears; exploring their hopes and wishes.

Encouraging self-worth

● **How good are you at emphasising the positives?**
  Neglected children will have experienced very little praise, but rather have been subjected to criticism/restrictions. Praise and emphasis of their good points show that they are not all bad, and helps to raise self-esteem.

● **Can you help the child begin to explore themselves?**
  Some children may never have been taught about their own bodies. This is a difficult area of work but can be done using books, physical activities/games. Opportunities for the child to realise their potential through physical and other activities help them learn about different senses and explore their environment.

● **Do you know of other ways to help the child explore their senses?**
  Games, toys and other play materials can help the child discover and enjoy their sensory system.

● **Can you provide opportunities for the child to explore their environment?**
  Bearing in mind their stage of development (i.e. nothing dangerous or beyond their capabilities), the child should be allowed to explore and develop an understanding of time, natural growth and their own physical activities.

- **How good are you at helping the child channel their aptitudes and interests?**
  Focus on the child's expressed interests and abilities, and encourage activities encompassing these that the child can carry through into adulthood, e.g. sport, music.
- **Can you help the child free their imagination?**
  This can be done through fantasy, play, music, painting and writing.
- **Can you give the child permission to enjoy themselves?**
  Speaks for itself – allow messiness in play, etc.

(Developed by Jane Asquith, BAAF)

Dan Hughes (2006) uses the term PACE to describe the key components of parenting that ensure that the parent or carer remains emotionally engaged with the child. PACE stands for Playfulness, Acceptance, Curiosity and Empathy. Although PACE was developed as part of a therapeutic intervention for building attachment between a child and their parent or carer, this framework or attitude can be adapted to direct work with children. The key message to give to the child is that you are available, attentive and tuned in to their needs. A playful attitude can help to relax a child and to build a connection between child and worker; playfulness helps children learn that they can have fun. Understanding and acceptance of the child's emotions and behaviour can convey a message of acceptance: that the child is valued for who they are. A sense of curiosity about the child demonstrates that you hold them in your mind and that you are interested in helping them find ways of making sense of their behaviour, making connections between cause and effect and finding more appropriate ways of behaving. Empathy with the child can bring you closer together and help the child develop a sense of security in the knowledge that you understand them.

Before you start working with the child, think about what you know about them

Each child is unique with different personality characteristics, history and abilities. As you become familiar with the child's history and circumstances and get to know them, it will become easier to find an approach that works best for the child and yourself. Think about some of the following.

- How old is the child? Distinguish between chronological and developmental age. What do you know about their development (consider physical, emotional, cognitive, social and behavioural)?
- Does the child have any impairments? These might include sight, speech or hearing difficulties, learning difficulties, attention deficit hyperactivity disorder (ADHD), Asperger's syndrome or autism, Foetal Alcohol Effects (FAE).
- What is the child's sense of identity? What factors should be taken into consideration relating to their ethnicity, culture, religion, language, gender, disability or sexuality?
- What is the child's attachment history, and what are the implications of this for their ability to trust and communicate with adults?
- What are the significant events in the child's life? Draw a timeline or flowchart to help you picture the child's life and understand the potential impact of different events on relationships and development.
- What is the child interested in? Can you begin to develop a relationship with the child through their interests?

Have a range of tools and methods available for working with children and young people

There is now a wide range of books, toys and other resources available for working with children and young people. Many of these have been devised for children who have been hurt in some way. It's a good idea to build up a set of resources that can be shared by you and your team.

Activities designed to build rapport can include sharing food, or connecting through using the senses, for example, experimenting with different tastes and smells (Stringer, 2009, pp 18–20). Activities around the five senses, including sand and water play, are often a useful precursor to addressing feelings. The *Bear Cards* (www.incentiveplus. co.uk; available from BAAF), which represent through cartoon characters a range of feelings, can be a fun way of exploring emotions. Safe ways can be found for children to express their anger, for instance, story books, bean bags or punch bags, drawing and painting, use of puppets, etc (Corrigan and Moore, 2011).

Activities which help children to explore relationships include using puppets, dolls and dolls' houses, and worksheets to help children represent their home, their relationships, their fears, hopes and wishes. Parent message cards (Fahlberg, 1994) can be used to talk about parents and parenting and how this has impacted on the child's feelings about themselves.

> *Over the weeks I spent alone, with myself and a woman who only got up to buy some more beer and drink herself back into a coma that would last from one to three days, I did realise that something was wrong with her. I also realised there was nothing I could do. So I did what I could for myself. I got drinks by climbing onto the kitchen table and pouring the contents of a bottle into a dirty glass, which I used repeatedly. I could get nothing to eat as food was in the fridge and the handle was out of reach. So I would wait for my mother to resurface, still drunk, stagger from her room and bring me a plate of cheese and crackers every few days, if she remembered.*
>
> *(Francis Davis, at age 16, quoted in Harris, 2008, p 16)*

Helping children to talk about how their needs have or have not been met can be facilitated by using the brick wall technique (see Corrigan and Moore, 2011). This is a useful metaphor for helping children understand why people have been concerned about the care they have been receiving from their parents. You will need a box of bricks, each with a picture or word representing a particular need. A wall is built with the bricks, and as it is built the worker describes all the things children need to be safe and for healthy growth. As the child begins to talk about the lack of food, cuddles, routines, etc, the relevant bricks are removed. The wall is undermined and eventually falls down. The use of metaphor is often helpful in work with children as it allows the child to maintain a safe distance from the pain of his own experiences.

Publications that provide some useful examples of direct work techniques include *Communicating with Vulnerable Children* (Corrigan and Moore, 2011) and *Communicating through Play* (Stringer, 2009). A useful interactive resource is *In My Shoes* (www.inmyshoes.org.uk). For other helpful publications and resources, see below.

Key points

- Children and young people have a right to be listened to and their wishes and feelings taken into account in planning and decision-making.
- The child's voice can easily get lost in cases of neglect – be aware of the possible barriers to hearing the child.
- Neglected children are at risk of being unseen and unheard.
- Ask yourself 'What does this mean for the child?' (Helm, 2010, p 170)
- Ask yourself how confident you are that you have been able to ascertain the child's wishes and feelings.
- Always keep the child at the centre of your thinking.
- Practitioners need knowledge and skills for direct work with children and young people.
- Practitioners deserve good supervision, support and training in skills in working with children and young people.
- Direct work with children is supported by having a range of tools and resources.

Resources for working with children and young people

Resources for use with children

Sriker S and Kimmel E (1981) *The Anti-Colouring Book*, London: Scholastic

Williams M (1922) *The Velveteen Rabbit, or how Toys become Real*, London: Random House

53

Wilson, Jacqueline – children's fiction relating to children living in a range of family situations and managing change in their lives. Titles include:

The Story of Tracey Beaker
The Dare Game
Double Act
Bad Girls
Dustbin Baby
The Suitcase Kid
The Bread and Breakfast Star

In My Shoes: interactive computer package to help children and vulnerable adults communicate about experiences and relationships – visit www.inmyshoes.org.uk.

Resources for practitioners

CAFCASS, *My Needs, Wishes and Feelings Pack* (designed to help children describe how significant harm is affecting their lives – visit www.cafcass.gov.uk/publications.aspx)

Corrigan M and Moore J (2011) *Communicating with Vulnerable Children*, London: BAAF

Dalzell R and Chamberlain C (2006) *Communicating with Children during Assessment: Training pack*, London: NCB

Gilligan R (2001) *Promoting Resilience: A resource guide on working with children in the care system*, London: BAAF

Jewett C (1994) *Helping Children Cope with Separation and Loss* (2nd edn), London: Free Association Books

Mencap (2003) *Listen Up: Helping children with a learning disability complain about the services they use*, London: Mencap (a video resource pack designed to help children with a learning disability, including those with profound and multiple learning disabilities, express their views and feelings on the services they use. Contains children's workbooks; a CD-ROM to help users customise posters; complaints cards and parents' leaflets; a staff training video and workbook on using the materials)

NSPCC, *How It Is* (an image vocabulary developed with Triangle to help children communicate about a range of issues – particularly useful for disabled children. Visit www.nspcc.org.uk)

Regan, L, Pelling C and Jones S (2002) *Looking Glass: A positive communication workbook*, Lyme Regis: Russell House Publishing

Stringer B (2009) *Communicating through Play: Techniques for assessing and preparing children for adoption*, London: BAAF

TIP 5

Understand the impact of neglect on children

Child neglect is a serious form of maltreatment that can have significant effects on all areas of child development with long-term consequences. In the most severe cases, children can die.

Egeland *et al* (1981, 1983) found that where children were both neglected and had 'psychologically unavailable' parents, they were likely to be anxiously attached to their primary caregivers and show signs of pathological behaviours. These included 'unusual sexual behaviours; wetting or soiling, excessive appetite, repetitive movements such as rocking and self-punishing behaviours' (Egeland *et al*, 1983, quoted in Stevenson, 2007, p 74). Self-efficacy and self-esteem are also likely to be affected. The impact of physical neglect can also be devastating, whether it is the infant left in urine-soaked bedding with the risk of serious infection, or the malnourished child whose growth is compromised and who is in a constant state of stress and anxiety.

> **9.12 Severe neglect of young children has adverse effects on children's ability to form attachments and is associated with major impairment of growth and intellectual development. Persistent neglect can lead to serious impairment of health and development, and long-term difficulties with social functioning, relationships and educational progress. Neglected children may also experience low self-esteem, and feelings of being unloved and isolated. Neglect can also result, in extreme cases, in death. The impact of neglect varies depending on how long children have been neglected, the children's age, and the multiplicity of neglectful behaviours children have been experiencing.**
>
> *(DCSF, 2010)*

The impact of neglect on the child's developmental needs

Health	Failure to thrive, developmental delay, dental caries, illnesses and infections, lack of immunisation, substance misuse, unsafe sexual activity
Education	Poor play skills, delayed speech and language development, low academic achievement, poor cognitive skills, poor school attendance, misconduct at school, compromised employment opportunities

Emotional and behavioural development	Anxious or disordered attachments, lack of empathy, inability to manage stress, inability to control impulses, conduct disorder, withdrawn, aggressive
Identity	Poor self-image and self-esteem, lack of sense of belonging, negative impact on ethnic and cultural identity
Family and social relationships	Poor peer relationships, isolated, subject to bullying and rejection by peers, lack of appropriate adult role models
Social presentation	Dirty, smelly, lack of appropriate clothing impacting on social relationships and sense of belonging, lack of involvement in community
Self-care skills	Lack of problem-solving skills, overly dependent, self-reliant and inappropriately independent, lack of confidence and competence

See also Horwath (2007b, pp 50–51), for the impact of neglect on child development.

Consider neglect from an attachment perspective

Most children develop strategies for ensuring their attachment needs are met. These patterns of attachment develop from the child–caregiver interactions, in particular the way in which the parent or caregiver responds to the child's expression of need. The child whose parent is available and responds in a consistent, sensitive and nurturing manner is likely to develop a secure attachment. They will be open and trusting, able to express a range of feelings and develop appropriate independence. The child who, in the main, cannot be sure of a sensitive, attuned response will develop an anxious attachment. Where parenting is cold, rejecting and controlling, the child learns to suppress the expression of emotional need and becomes self-reliant and compliant. This is typical of an anxious-avoidant pattern of attachment. The child with an anxious-ambivalent pattern of attachment experiences the parent as insensitive to their needs, inconsistent in response to need and often preoccupied with their own problems. They can become an attention-seeking, clingy and angry child.

These are organised patterns of attachment: behaviour is organised around strategies for ensuring attention from the parent or caregiver. The child with a disorganised pattern of attachment is one who has been unable to find a safe way of getting attention from their parent. These are children who often live in violent and abusive households; they experience their parent as frightening and dangerous on the one hand and frightened and helpless on the other. Life for these children can be chaotic, confusing and full of fear.

Howe (2005) uses an attachment framework to make sense of the caregiving relationship in cases of abuse and neglect. He considers different types of neglect and their impact on the developing child. The following is a summary of Howe's attachment perspective.

Disorganised neglect

Disorganised neglect: parents live from crisis to crisis; feelings dominate and motivate behaviour; the family appears to be always on the verge of disaster; practitioners' time is hijacked to meet parents' needs; the family lives in chaos.

The inconsistent and unreliable nature of parental response leads to these children developing a strategy to ensure that they receive attention. Children living in these environments are demanding, irritable and loud. Their behaviour is very attention-seeking and they are difficult to soothe. Their capacity to concentrate is limited and they can be disruptive in school because of their need always to be at the centre of the teacher's attention. Peer relationships are difficult due to jealousy and anger and their exaggerated behaviour. By the time these children reach adolescence they can be out of their parents' control, their immaturity and impulsivity leading to anti-social behaviour.

Depressed, passive neglect

Depressed, passive neglect: parents defend against thoughts and feelings; they appear withdrawn and dull, they lack motivation; they neither perceive the child's needs nor do they believe in their own or others' effectiveness; they have developed "learned helplessness".

Living in a lifeless, depressed environment with little communication between adult and child, these children give up and close down. They may engage in self-soothing activities such as rocking or become detached from the world around them. Some engage in role reversal and take on a caring role towards the parent.

Their home environment is often run-down, dirty and unkempt. A sense of hopelessness and depression pervades the atmosphere. Children are left to their own devices with little or no supervision. They appear listless and disinterested. Infants despair of anyone responding to their cries, so give up. At school, they are often alone, unable to join in; they make no effort to learn because they lack belief in their ability. They are vulnerable to teasing and bullying if they are dirty and smelly.

Emotional neglect and abuse

Emotional neglect and abuse: often referred to as "psychological maltreatment"; parents recognise the child's need but either wilfully or defensively fail to respond; may reject in a hostile manner; the child is there to meet others' needs. The atmosphere is cold, with an underlying anger.

Children living in this environment, with unavailable parents, lack the opportunity to explore and understand their own and others' emotions. These children are unhappy and distressed. They have to take care of themselves, sometimes appearing precocious. Their behaviour becomes anti-social, they are disruptive and under-achieve at school, become either isolated and withdrawn or aggressive and hostile. They do not seek comfort when distressed, displaying either an avoidant or disorganised attachment pattern. When these children reach adolescence, they display a range of delinquent and self-harming behaviours.

These are children who have been traumatised by psychological maltreatment. High levels of anxiety and stress can affect their brain development and have long-lasting consequences.

(You may also meet situations of emotional neglect masked by well-organised households that offer children many material advantages and opportunities for achievement, but where there is a lack of emotional connection between parent and child or emotional rejection.)

Severe deprivation and chronic neglect

Severe deprivation and chronic neglect: a feature of inadequate institutional care; parents are depressed or uninterested, with significant problems of their own; children passed from one "carer" to another; parents lack curiosity, leaving the child alone.

Children who have suffered chronic neglect and have failed to develop selective attachments have been left alone to manage their own needs. They are in a state of high arousal and distress, unable either to understand their senses or to regulate their emotions. They will "attach" themselves to anyone who expresses interest. The longer these children remain in environments of chronic neglect, the more severe the long-term effects. These children often exhibit symptoms associated with attachment disorder:

- *impulsivity;*
- *very poor relationships, including peer rejection;*
- *educational problems;*
- *hyperactivity, restlessness and attention deficits;*
- *delayed language development;*
- *cognitive impairments (seriously affecting their academic performance);*
- *aggressive and coercive behaviours;*
- *eating problems (usually eating too much voraciously).*

(Howe, 2005, p 145)

Attachment disorder can be expressed through the child being either emotionally withdrawn – *inhibited*, or indiscriminately social – *disinhibited* (Zeanah, 1996, cited in Howe, 2005). The inhibited child is withdrawn and passive with little interest in the world around them. Some display symptoms similar to autism, for example, rhythmic movements, rocking and head banging. The disinhibited child will go to anyone, including strangers, for attention, will be clingy and attention-seeking and unaware of appropriate personal boundaries. Their interaction with others is superficial and they have difficulties with peer relationships. Their development is impaired in three areas:

> *...interpersonal relationships, impulse control and the regulation of aggression. There is a long-term incapacity to establish emotionally meaningful relationships. Notions of reciprocity and mutuality are lacking. As these children progress through childhood, rates of criminal behaviour, anger, interpersonal conflict, poor concentration and problems with school increase.*
>
> (Howe, 2005, pp 147–48)

Be aware of the impact of neglect on early brain development

In the last decade or so, we have learnt a lot about the impact of abuse and neglect on the developing brain of the infant and small child, and this has influenced UK child care policy and practice. Understanding the mechanisms and processes of early brain development can help you understand the impact of neglect on early development and the need to act quickly where very young children are concerned.

Babies are born with over 100 billion neurones (nerve cells) which provide the basic structure of the brain. The brain develops through connections (synapses) made between these neurones. The synaptic connections, their amount and strength, depend on the baby's environment.

Brain development

Brain stem	**Pre-birth to eight months** State regulation, heart rate, blood pressure, body temperature
Midbrain	**Birth to one year** Motor functioning and regulation, arousal, appetite and satiety
Limbic system	**Six months to two years** Emotional functioning, attachment and sexual behaviour
Cortex	**One year to four years** Cognitive functioning, concrete and abstract thought

The process of brain growth is sequential. Researchers believe that during the early years there exist "sensitive periods" for the development of certain capacities. The most rapid development of synapses occurs during these periods, providing almost limitless opportunities for learning (Child Welfare Information Gateway, 2001). After the age of three, if the synapses and neuronal pathways are not activated repeatedly, they will be pruned and lost. The optimal time for learning and development of capacities will be passed; this does not mean that learning cannot occur later on but it is likely to be more difficult.

Babies who are exposed in the ante-natal period to drugs or alcohol may be born with a reduced number of neurones and altered cortical development. The consequences of this can be difficulties with attention, memory and thought processes later on (for example, the child with Foetal Alcohol Spectrum Disorder or Foetal Alcohol Effects). Malnutrition, in the womb and in the first three years of life, can affect brain growth and the speed of brain signals. Severe malnutrition can result in cognitive, social and behavioural difficulties.

Babies need attuned caregivers who interact with them in order to begin to develop speech and language skills. Although born with a predisposition to form attachments, the lack of a sensitive and responsive caregiver in the first two years of life can seriously disrupt the attachment process in the infant and can have long-lasting effects on the child's capacity to form healthy relationships later on.

Global neglect, such as is seen in environments of severe deprivation, for example, some of the orphanages in China and Romania, can have a devastating effect on all aspects of development, although "catch up" is possible if the child is placed in a nurturing environment in early infancy (Rutter *et al*, 2009). Chronic neglect can mean that a child is living in a persistent state of stress and hyper-arousal. Stress and trauma affect the neurochemistry of the brain and can significantly alter the patterns that are laid down, affecting physiological, social, emotional, cognitive and behavioural functioning.

Without an opportunity for proper nurturing in the early years, children's development can be compromised. When considering the impact of the environment on the young child's development, take into account the child's age, the quality of the care they are receiving during "sensitive periods" and the potential effects of lost opportunities for development and learning.

Don't forget the adolescent brain

There is another important period for brain development during adolescence, particularly affecting the pre-frontal cortex. The pre-frontal cortex is responsible for impulse control, planning and decision-making. During this period, teenagers are more likely to respond with "gut reactions", to seek out novelty and to engage in risk-taking behaviour. This is a time when teenagers need the support of adult guidance. The young person who has grown up in a neglectful environment is especially at risk. Hicks and Stein (2010) describe the effects of neglect on teenagers across the five outcomes of *Every Child Matters*. These include poor physical and mental health, suicide attempts, drug and alcohol misuse, early sexual activity, running away, being bullied, poor behaviour and academic achievement at school, and anti-social behaviour.

Reunification with birth parents is sometimes considered for older children on the basis of their ability to "look out" for themselves. This should be assessed carefully. Where the young person has experienced neglect, they may never have developed the capacity to manage their emotions and impulses and they may be returning to caregivers who are unable to provide the boundaries and supervision appropriate to their age and stage of development.

Be aware of the impact of parental factors on children's well-being

My name is Jane. I have Foetal Alcohol Syndrome. I have it because my mother was an alcoholic. My speech, hearing, auditory processing, my heart and stomach were affected. I spent a month in intensive care with projectile vomiting, bowel infection and a heart murmur …

I am healthy now but the long-lasting effect has been on my brain. My auditory processing is very slow and I also have trouble with my memory. This means that I can only follow one instruction at a time and I often quickly forget what I'm supposed to be doing. I only hear one in three words so I take a long time to respond. This means friendships are difficult because I have trouble following group conversations.

(Jane, age 17, quoted in Harris, 2008, p 41)

There is a higher risk of maltreatment to children living in families where there is domestic violence, mental illness, drug or alcohol misuse. Not all parents who use drugs or alcohol maltreat their children; some are able to prioritise their children's needs. When you are assessing the impact of these factors, consider whether there are any signs of protective mechanisms, for example, good parenting from the other parent, or a relative who can provide a secure base and a place of safety.

Children living with domestic violence are at an increased risk of:

- physical injury, including injury to the unborn child and particular vulnerability of the baby-in-arms;
- distress and anxiety;
- lack of sense of safety and security;
- emotional and behavioural disturbance as a result of witnessing violence to another person, often their mother;
- loneliness;
- poor social relationships.

Children who live with parental mental illness are at increased risk of:

- poor attachment relationship;
- inconsistent and emotionally unavailable parenting;
- behavioural problems;
- withdrawal, fantasising;
- emotional and behavioural difficulties in adolescence, including conduct disorder and depression;
- interrupted education;
- having to become a carer for their parent;
- poor social relationships; fewer opportunities to pursue leisure interests.

Children who live with parents who misuse drugs and/or alcohol are at increased risk of:

- damage to the developing foetus;
- withdrawal symptoms as a newborn; Foetal Alcohol Spectrum Disorder or Foetal Alcohol Effects;
- poor attachment relationship, lack of warmth and stimulation, negativity;
- violent behaviour from the parent;
- disrupted education, poor cognitive and intellectual development;
- physical neglect;
- having to become a carer for their parent;
- poor social relationships, loneliness and isolation;
- loss of childhood;
- early drug or alcohol use in adolescence.

Children who live with parents with learning disabilities are at increased risk of:

- neglect of their basic needs;
- poor cognitive development;
- lack of routines and safety;
- poor diet and hygiene, impacting on health, social relationships and sense of isolation;
- poor self-image;
- anxiety from inconsistent parenting;
- assuming a caring role in relation to the parent;
- lack of boundaries and supervision.

Key points

- The impact of neglect can be seen across all areas of child development.
- Chronic neglect will affect the structure and early development of the infant's brain.
- Neglect affects the development and pattern of attachment relationships.
- Both physical and mental health can be affected by neglect; low self-esteem is common amongst children and young people who have been neglected.
- Neglect affects cognitive ability leading to poor academic achievement and problems with conduct.
- There is an increased risk of substance misuse amongst young people who have been neglected.
- Child neglect can have a negative impact on adult relationships and parenting capacity.

TIP 6

Understand why parents neglect their children and identify signs of risk

We should not seek to understand the problem of neglectful parents solely in terms of external pressures on them, but rather in terms of individual and family dynamics, with external pressures as (often powerful) contributing factors.

(Stevenson, 2007, p 45)

The daily, unremitting grind of poverty and "social exclusion" and the stress and anxiety these cause will undoubtedly affect parents' ability to focus on the needs of their children. We cannot ignore socio-economic factors or other external factors, such as the support available from wider family, community and the state and the impact these have on parenting. However, to understand the mechanisms that operate we need to look at the *interaction* of these factors with the characteristics of the individual parent and family.

Research tells us that there are particular risk factors associated with child maltreatment. These factors are likely to be cumulative and raise the possibility of harm but cannot predict its occurrence. These factors are listed below.

- *Lone motherhood*
- *Young mothers*
- *Isolated mothers*
- *Larger families, more pregnancies and unplanned pregnancies*
- *Premature or very low birth weight baby*
- *Low income families*
- *Unemployed carers*
- *Carers with low educational attainment*
- *Relationships featuring domestic violence or high levels of conflict*
- *Substance misusing parents or carers*
- *Parental mental health problems, including maternal depression*
- *Personal history of childhood maltreatment*
- *Insecure attachment patterns in own childhood*
- *Maternal low self-esteem*
- *Families that are less cohesive and poorly organised, with little positive interactions between parents/carers and their children*
- *Parents/carers lacking sensitivity or responsiveness towards their children*

    (Moran, 2009, p 9)

Moran considers the young, depressed mother. Her lack of responsiveness to her child is understood in the context of her low self-esteem, isolation, unemployment and low income. Indicators of risk are useful signs but to understand the causal processes we need to consider the mechanisms at work (2009, p 8). We know that not all parents living in poverty maltreat their children, but we also know that the majority of parents who do maltreat their children are living in poverty. We need to ask ourselves: 'Why is it that this parent, living in these circumstances, is neglecting their child?'

> *Parents who have enjoyed more sensitive and psychologically available relationships during their own development tend to have more complex, differentiated and nuanced understandings of their own and other people's thoughts, feelings and behaviour.*
>
> *(Brandon et al, 2008, p 59)*

Consider the parents' history and how it affects their parenting capacity

You will need to take a full family and social history. This will help place child neglect in the context of individual and wider family functioning. A full history should include childhood experiences, significant events in their lives, previous and current relationships, their education and health histories, record of employment, parenting experience and history of involvement with different agencies. Think about what meaning their history has to the parent and how they see themselves.

Adult attachment theory is based on the premise that how adults *think* and *feel* about their early relationships is strongly related to the quality of the attachment relationship which develops with their own children. Adults who have experienced secure attachment relationships as children are more able to engage in mutually satisfying relationships and, as parents, are able to tune into their child's feeling, thinking and behaviour in a sensitive way.

Common to the lives of many parents who neglect their children are childhood histories of instability and insecurity, hostile or abusive parenting and lack of nurturing. For those who fail to experience as they grow up any positive mediating factors, such as another adult taking an interest in their lives, the pattern of instability and unsatisfactory relationships continues into adulthood and parenting.

> *'Victims of neglect who do not repeat the cycle have fewer stressful life events; stronger, more stable and supportive relationships with husbands and boyfriends; physically healthier babies.' They are also 'less likely to be maltreated by both parents and more apt to have reported a supportive relationship with one parent or with another child. These mediating factors provide critical indicators for improving parents' potential'.*
>
> (Gaudin, 1993, quoted in Stevenson, 2007, p 47)

Not all parents who have experienced maltreatment in their early lives go on to abuse or neglect their own children. Factors that mediate these experiences will include inherited characteristics, for example, sociability and attractiveness; other adults who provide a sense of safety and security in childhood; a relationship with a partner that provides "earned security"; and capacity for insight and reflection.

They must be able to mentally process the attachment signals from their child, and be able to respond at the four levels Crittenden (1993) talks about: hearing the child; interpreting the child; believing they can respond; and responding effectively.

Look for connections between the parents' past and present and what this means for parenting

When listening to how parents tell their stories, consider the following.

● Are they able to acknowledge both negative and positive experiences during their childhood? Do they show appropriate levels of feeling when talking about difficult or painful experiences?

- Can they reflect on childhood experiences? Do they have insight into the effect of childhood experiences on the adult/parent they are today? Do they tend to dismiss the impact of traumatic events, or do they seem overly preoccupied with these? Are they aware that others, i.e. their parents, may have had a different perspective on what happened to them?
- Are they able to tell their story in a coherent manner? In other words, does the story make sense; does it "fit together" or does it contradict itself; do the answers they give reflect the questions asked?
- Have they been able to process earlier trauma or loss? To what extent have they managed to resolve earlier losses? Have they arrived at a level of acceptance; can they separate past feelings from present hopes and desires; has the intensity of feelings of loss been transformed into a sense of sadness or regret; have they managed to take something positive from the earlier loss?
- During their lives, have they been able to develop close confiding relationships – with a parent, a supportive adult, a friend, a partner?
- Do they have a support network? Are they able to seek and use support appropriately? Can they offer help and support to others?

The secure adult will demonstrate the above capacities and is more likely to promote a secure attachment with their child. The parent who dismisses or minimises the effect of negative childhood experiences, or the parent who seems still to be preoccupied with these events, is at risk of promoting anxious and insecure attachments in their children. Where the parent has unresolved issues of trauma or loss, the child who triggers traumatic and stressful memories of unmet childhood needs is a child potentially at risk. The parent who was themselves abused or neglected as a child may feel overwhelmed by the child's dependence on them and retreat into a sense of helplessness and hopelessness or alternatively, respond with anger and rage.

Assess current functioning as a parent

Think about how the parents understand and manage social relationships. How does this impact on the relationship of care? Can they recognise and understand their child's feelings, thinking and behaviour and adjust their expectations and caretaking behaviour in response? Can they empathise with their child? Are their expectations of the child realistic? Are their expectations mainly positive or negative? Do they have difficulty in mentally processing signals from the child? Try to identify where the problem lies. What could be done to change things? Simply instructing parents on what they should be doing is unlikely to be sufficient. It relies on the parent's capacity for empathy, their understanding of how children of different ages express their needs, the meaning they give to their child's behaviour, being flexible in their response and the ability to focus on the child's needs first and foremost.

Consider how the parent feels about themselves. Low self-esteem is a common factor in neglectful mothers. It can also be a feature of depression. It may reflect a lack of nurturing in their earlier and current lives. Observe the parent's behaviour, how they refer to themselves and their lives, their responses to advice and help. Stevenson (2007) encapsulates the mindset of the depressed mother in this quotation.

> *'If I am not loved, then I am not worthy of love. It follows that there is no point in seeking to make myself attractive to others, either through appearance or responses. Even my house can be dirty like me; my children, who are, after all, bits of me, need not (cannot) be cherished. As for men, they are allowed to exploit me; maybe because this is how men always were in my family and because I do not deserve anything better.'*
>
> *(Stevenson, 2007, p 49)*

Gender issues are important. Caring is still generally seen to be women's work. Stevenson (2007) reminds us that some women may not want to be mothers or, at least, may feel ambivalent about their role. They may recall their own mothers' negativity and sense of drudgery; they may have hoped for more from being a parent and been left with a sense of disappointment because becoming a parent has not filled the gap left by their own unmet needs. Fathers may be absent, difficult to engage with and, in some cases, dangerous. There is an insidious power exerted over women by those men who impregnate them and move on to the next woman.

Consider the parents' current lifestyle and the implications for child neglect

Domestic violence, drug and alcohol misuse and parental learning disability figure largely in the family lives of neglected children. The impact of each will depend on a range of variables including the extent of the problem, parental acknowledgement of the problem, personality characteristics, the capacity of the parent to prioritise the child's needs and access appropriate services, and the resilience of the individual child. The bottom line must always be the lived experience of the child and the impact on their overall development. We know that many children whose lives include domestic violence and/or substance misuse do not have their basic needs met, are isolated, ashamed, unhappy, fearful and anxious, and often live in dangerous surroundings.

Domestic violence

The safety and welfare of children is undermined by exposure to domestic violence. Domestic violence rarely occurs in isolation, but is often accompanied by drug or alcohol misuse, poor physical and mental health and poor childhood experiences (DCSF, 2010). It can impact on mothers' parenting capacity by undermining their mental health, their self-respect and their authority to parent. They may experience lack of confidence, depression, a sense of degradation and sleep problems. Mothers sometimes prioritise their partners' needs in order to protect themselves and their children from further violence.

Mental illness

Depression and anxiety are common to many mothers who neglect their children. Depression can cause a sense of worthlessness and helplessness that leads to neglect of self and children. Mental health problems are often associated with drug or alcohol misuse, with personality disorder and significant physical illness (DCSF, 2010). There may be serious risks from the delusional thoughts of a parent suffering from a psychotic illness. Post-natal depression will hamper a mother's capacity to respond to her infant's needs. Mood swings can result in inconsistent parenting. The impact of mental illness will vary hugely from one parent to another and will also depend on the treatment and support available, including a supportive partner. It is important to look at these factors when considering the impact of mental illness on parenting capacity.

Problem drug and alcohol use

One cannot generalise the effects of drug misuse – it will depend on the type of drug, the amount used, the individual's tolerance of it and other characteristics related to the user. Problematic drug use usually occurs over time and, for those coming off drugs, relapse is common. Drug misuse is often associated with child maltreatment. Parents have difficulty organising their own and their children's lives. Basic needs are unmet; parents are emotionally unavailable to their children; they are unable to provide appropriate behavioural control and boundaries. Children are often left to fend for themselves. Faced with debt, and sometimes criminal activity, to fund their drug habit, parents can undermine family stability.

Some parents who use drugs are able to prioritise their children's needs. The impact of parental drug use can be reduced if they use the support services available to them and their children.

The impact of problem drinking will depend on the quantity consumed, the parent's level of tolerance, their current mental state and personality factors. In men, alcohol misuse is often associated with violence; in women, with neglect. It can affect sleep patterns, cause inappropriate behaviour and lack of inhibition, lack of motor co-ordination – all impacting on the ability to meet basic needs. Children most at risk are those where alcohol and violence feature together. Chronic problem drinking is often associated with relapse.

> *It's strange how I can still remember the three promises she gave me when I was growing up. Still a toddler about three years old, but I still remember:*
>
> *'I promise you I will always look after you.*
>
> *I will always care and I will never hit you.'*
>
> *She broke all three. With the days and nights of continuous drinking and sleeping, the small lapses in between, where she would stagger around drunkenly looking for another can, she broke every promise she made to me.*
>
> (Francis Davis, at age 16, quoted in Harris, 2008, pp 14–15)

Learning disability

There is no direct link between parents' learning disability and wilful neglect, although it may be associated with neglect by omission (DCSF, 2010). A child is more likely to be at risk where learning disabled parents have additional stressors, such as a disabled child, financial difficulties, domestic violence, substance misuse, poor health, social isolation or poor childhood experiences. For some learning disabled parents, their capacity to meet basic needs is compromised by the inability to understand new or complex information and learn new skills. They may be unable to provide appropriate stimulation, protect a child from danger and understand the child's changing developmental needs. Their reduced ability to cope independently affects the child's social functioning, and presents professionals with huge dilemmas about appropriate levels of intervention to support families.

How can practitioners engage with resistant parents?

Secrecy, denial and resistance are common challenges to social care practitioners working with neglectful parents. Finding a way that encourages parents to be open about their problems at the same time as maintaining a safeguarding function can be difficult. There is a tendency for child protection social work to be high on confrontation and low on listening. An approach that is more client-centred and less confrontational, one based on principles of empathy, being non-judgemental and client-centred can help to reduce resistance (Forrester *et al*, 2006). However, the dilemma for child protection workers is that the approach must contain direction, with the focus clearly on the safety of the child. Concepts such as working in partnership are difficult to put into practice when the goals of the parents diverge from the need to protect the child.

The challenge for practitioners is to develop an approach to working with parents that is honest and clear in identifying the problems and the required outcomes without creating hostility; an approach that is empathic without colluding with parents. Such a strategy depends on focusing, where possible, on relationship-building and using more listening skills and less confrontation. At the same time, you need to bear in mind the significant group of parents who are hostile and resistant to the intervention of professional agencies. They will engage in manipulation and subterfuge. At all times, you have to maintain a healthy scepticism and resist accepting the parent's word without evidence to support it.

Parents who maltreat their children rarely signal their need for help in direct ways. There are, however, signs that should alert you to the possibility of difficulties. Parents may make frequent visits with the child to the GP or A&E departments, or to children's social care offices. They may voice concerns or questions about their ability to parent; they may ask whether their parenting might harm the child or directly express fear of harming them.

Key points

- Parents' neglect of their children is usually the result of an interaction of personal, family, community and societal factors. Consider the parents' attachment history and how this impacts on their capacity to respond to their child.
- Try to understand the mother or father, their thinking and feeling in relation to being a parent.
- Consider the parents' own needs without allowing them to divert your attention away from your responsibility to safeguard and protect the child.

- Assess the impact of domestic violence, mental illness, learning disability and substance misuse on parenting capacity.
- Working with resistant parents requires an ability to balance working together in a non-confrontational way with the need to protect the child.

TIP 7

Consider different components of the assessment

The Common Assessment Framework (England) was designed for use by any professional who has concerns about a child with whom their work brings them into contact. The framework allows for the gathering of information about the child, including information from other agencies. Where the outcomes of the action plan following assessment are not achieved and concerns remain, the child is likely to be referred to children's social services and a core assessment undertaken. Where there are child protection concerns, a core assessment will form part of child protection procedures. This chapter focuses on some of the key aspects to consider when undertaking core assessments of children and families where neglect is the primary concern.

Assess using an ecological framework

The assessment of children and their families will be undertaken using *The Framework for the Assessment of Children in Need and their Families* (DH, 2000a) in England and Wales, and its equivalent in other UK countries (in Scotland, the *Framework for Standards for Professionals for Child Protection* (2004); in Northern Ireland, a number of frameworks are in use). A good ecological assessment does not simply collect data but must also be analytical, addressing the complex ways in which the three domains of the framework interact with one another. (There are a range of assessment tools to support the assessment framework, but beware of simply using these as checklists. Their value lies in being part of an in-depth, reflective and analytical assessment.) For instance, a family's entrenched and long-standing

Assessment framework

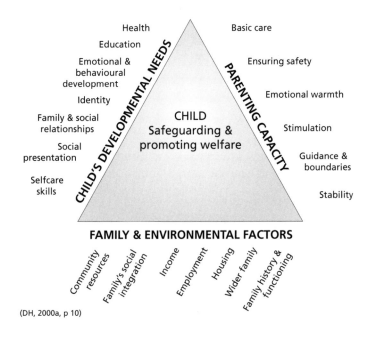

(DH, 2000a, p 10)

financial difficulties need to be viewed in relation to their hostility and resistance to engaging with services that might help them, and the effect of this on their ability to meet their children's needs.

Principles underpinning the assessment framework

Assessments:

- are child centred;
- are rooted in child development;
- are ecological in their approach;
- ensure equality of opportunity;
- involve working with children and families;
- build on strengths as well as identify difficulties;
- are inter-agency in their approach to assessment and the provision of services;
- are a continuing process, not a single event;
- are carried out in parallel with other action and providing services;
- are grounded in evidence-based knowledge.

(DH, 2000a, p 10)

Horwath draws our attention to a fourth domain in the assessment framework, one that influences the practitioner's approach to neglect cases.

> *...existing assessment frameworks and tools do not draw practitioners' attention to reflecting on how knowledge about a case is constructed and interpreted in light of a practitioner's personal, professional and organisational situation.*
>
> *(2007a, p 1287)*

Horwath suggests that the fourth domain should include the following dimensions:

Perception of child neglect and the evidence base for concerns;
Interpretation of professional role;
Perception of social work services;
Personal feelings;
Community role;
Perception of the team and manager.

(2007, p 1299)

Have a clear theoretical basis for the assessment and plan a framework

Calder and Hackett's stepwise model of assessment (2003, p 122) provides a useful framework for planning and carrying out the assessment and helps you develop hypotheses (ways of understanding) from an early stage.

Applying Calder and Hackett's model to assessing child neglect, consider the following.

- **Plan**
  Timescales are established. Issues of partnership, equality and power are addressed. Working relationships are established; barriers to communication and involvement addressed, including strategies for working with resistant parents. Consideration of ways to ensure the views of parents, children and others are heard. Multi-agency involvement in the assessment is established. Tasks and responsibilities for aspects of the assessment agreed. Criteria and thresholds for neglect are established.

- **Hypothesise**
  The assessor begins to generate hypotheses about family functioning and care of the child as information comes to light. Hypothesising includes the application of different theoretical frameworks, research evidence and practice wisdom to emerging information and observation. Hypothesising continues throughout the assessment, with the worker testing out different ways of understanding and being prepared to adjust and change their

judgements. The vulnerabilities of and risks to the child are considered.

● **Gather**
Information is gathered using different methods – interviews, observation, assessment tools and checklists, genograms, ecomaps, information from other professionals involved with the child and family. The child is seen and heard.

● **Test**
The validity and reliability of information gathered from different sources is checked. Gaps and inconsistencies are addressed. Parental co-operation is tested against evidence of motivation to change and engagement in change. Information and evidence are checked against existing and emerging hypotheses. Information is tested against assessor's and others' understanding of threshold for neglect.

● **Analyse and make judgements**
Information and evidence, including patterns of behaviour and parenting style, strengths, protective and risk factors, are analysed in relation to the child's developmental needs, vulnerabilities and risk of harm. Judgements are made on the basis of an in-depth assessment and analysis.

● **Decide plan**
A care plan is devised on the basis of the needs of the child and capacity of the parents to protect and promote the child's welfare. Where child protection investigations have not been instigated, the care plan ensures that the child does not continue to experience a low level of neglect.

(Adapted from Calder and Hackett, 2003)

Having a clear theoretical basis for the assessment – what Reder and Duncan (2004) refer to as the 'thinking' aspect of practice – provides a way of building hypotheses. You should consider how attachment theory, knowledge of child development, trauma theory, systems theory and resilience can help your understanding. Other useful frameworks and resources include C4EO Safeguarding briefing no. 3

(Burton, 2009) and its section on using hypotheses and analysis in the assessment of children in need; Horwath's (2005) framework for assessing child neglect; and Minty and Pattinson's (1994) *Scale of Assessing Neglectful Parenting*, reproduced in Stevenson (2007, pp 153–61). Horwath talks about the need for practitioners 'to act as detectives rather than barristers' (p 90): by this, she means that whereas the barrister will defend one point of view, detectives will search 'for the truth, keeping an open mind and testing the conclusions they reach' (2005, p 86).

Consider using a range of assessment tools

You may be familiar with the Signs of Safety assessment tool (Turnell and Edwards, 1999) which is now in use in a number of local authorities. This tool was devised to ensure that assessments are not based solely on risk but also identify strengths and signs of safety, and work on collaboration with parents or carers. The tool includes a number of practice principles which can be applied to building partnerships and focusing on change. These principles include respecting parents as people who can be worked with; acknowledging strengths as well as weaknesses; recognising that co-operation can be achieved even where coercion is necessary; acknowledging that all families will have some signs of safety; and ensuring a focus on safety. This model applies the principles of solution-focused approaches to highlight small changes and achievements. Where neglectful parents are often difficult to engage, this approach has some advantages. However, as with other strengths-based approaches, there is a risk that practitioners might adopt a "rule of optimism", focusing on small signs of co-operation or change whilst failing to see signs of risk or harm. The focus must always be on the child's lived experience.

The Graded Care Profile (Srivastava *et al*, 2003) is also becoming more widely used. This is a practical tool that allows the practitioner to measure different aspects of care on a graded scale. There are four areas of need based on Maslow's hierarchy of needs: physical needs; safety in the presence and absence of carer; love; and belongingness and esteem. Each area of need is broken down into descriptors of care. These descriptors can help improve understanding (by the family and professionals involved) about the level of concern and target areas of work. This tool can be used by an individual worker with a family or by the group of professionals around the family. Aspects of care and commitment are graded from 1 to 5. The Graded Care Profile allows for the monitoring of change, both positive and negative. Its objective nature and the detail of the descriptors of care means that this tool can be useful in identifying signs of neglect at an early stage, to monitor change, to evidence chronic neglect and agree thresholds for intervention.

Genograms and chronologies are also essential tools in assessment. A genogram can aid the identification of intergenerational patterns of relationships and behaviours.

> *The genogram is a diagrammatic representation of significant information about a family, such as sex, age, familial relationship, household composition, number and order of offspring, etc.*
>
> *(Reder et al, 1993, p 138)*

The genogram contains detailed data on relationships between family members. It goes beyond a traditional family tree by allowing you to analyse hereditary patterns and psychological factors that punctuate relationships. Genograms help you to identify and understand various patterns in the family history which may have had an influence on the current state of mind of different family members. A good genogram contains a wealth of information on the family and maps out relationships and traits, signs of risk and resilience. It will include siblings of the subject child living elsewhere. The genogram can help identify members of the wider family able to protect the child, as well as those who may pose a risk to the child. Genograms can be used to generate questions to aid understanding of family functioning, values and beliefs and cultural differences related to childcare.

Because neglect usually occurs over a period of time, signs can be missed unless you take an overview of the child's life. A good chronology reveals patterns of care and can be useful in identifying the impact of different interventions and the capacity of the family to make and sustain improvement. The single incidents, such as failure to attend a hospital follow-up appointment, or an injury sustained through lack of supervision, assume different meanings when seen in total. In the case of Khyra Ishaq (*SCR 14 Birmingham Children's Safeguarding Board*, a child who died in May 2008 as a result of starvation), there were a number of worrying signs from an early age: failed or cancelled appointments; reports of an abusive father; concerns about Khyra stealing food; refusal of entry to the home after the commencement of home schooling; and the mother's resistance to intervention.

The recorded comments of social workers or health visitors about the state of the home or failure to gain access to the child should raise concerns when they occur time after time. Patterns of self-referrals or referrals from professionals need to be analysed. A good chronology will contain more than just dates and facts – it will include detailed information and analysis, for example, of the developmental impact of particular events, the interaction of different incidents and the integration and analysis of information from different sources.

A range of tools were developed alongside the *Framework for the Assessment of Children and their Families*. The *Home Conditions*, *Adult Wellbeing* and *Alcohol Use* tools (www.dh.gov.uk) can be helpful if they are used to inform your analysis. They will not, however, help identify false compliance, and can only aid an assessment as part of a rigorous evidence-gathering and analytical process. Don't forget the role of observation and direct questioning.

Communicate with parents and other professionals

This section focuses on communicating with parents and the professional network. For more information on communicating with children, see Tip 4.

Communicating with parents

"Hard to reach" families are often afraid of being judged and it is not uncommon for practitioners working with neglectful families to meet with resistance, hostility and failure to engage with practitioners. The stigma of contact with social work services can prevent families from seeking help. It is important, therefore, to be skilled in communicating and to work towards establishing constructive and empathic relationships with parents, acknowledging their ambivalence and the difficulties they may have in managing social relationships. Showing interest in parents' lives and their difficulties can result in insights into the psychological and emotional barriers that prevent them from engaging with professionals. Exhorting a mother to change her behaviour may have little effect without first exploring her own history and how this has shaped her parenting and ability to meet the needs of her child.

Remember that it is the parents and children who are best able to describe to you what their lives are like. In relation to cultural issues, it is important to be sensitive to difference, to overcome concerns about being seen as racist and to approach families with respect and a curiosity in finding out about their different cultural practices in child rearing (Stevenson, 2007) and how these are reflected in family functioning. You need to ask yourself about the potential vulnerability of certain groups of children, for example, those who are disabled. You also need to consider how some families will feel about sharing confidential information outside their family or community network and how this might affect the assessment.

Working together with the professional network

A true picture of child neglect will only emerge when information is brought together by all the different services involved with the family. Inter-agency collaboration is essential, with all services acknowledging their safeguarding responsibilities and working together. This means avoiding a "silo" mentality where services work in isolation, overcoming professional jealousies and status issues, and being clear about when and how to share information (DCSF, 2006a). Health visitors have a key safeguarding role with infants and pre-school children; teachers and other school staff will be in a position to identify signs of concern in school. Workers in adult services, including services for mental health, drug and alcohol, domestic violence, probation officers, the police and housing services can all contribute information about parents' lifestyles that will enhance the understanding of the child's experience and needs.

In their practice guide on working with adolescents who have been neglected, Hicks and Stein mention seven "enablers" of inter-agency working that managers and practitioners should focus on.

- *Understanding and respecting the role and responsibility of other services*
- *Good communication*
- *Regular contact and meetings*
- *Common priorities and trust*
- *Joint training*
- *Knowing what services are available and who to contact*
- *Clear guidelines and procedures for working together*

   (2010, p 21)

Putting collaboration into practice is the responsibility of everyone. The time and effort you put into forging good working relationships, including face-to-face conversations and regular contact, will ensure better safeguarding of children and young people.

Assess parental co-operation and resistance

We know that in many cases of neglect, parental resistance is a factor that makes it more difficult for practitioners to gain access to the child and to form a true picture of what is going on. Levels of co-operation or resistance are not static or uniform. One parent may be prepared to co-operate with professionals where another is not. Parents may work more willingly with some services (often those without the power to remove their children) than others. Families may accept outside involvement sometimes and not at other times, and some will be more resistant than others. Be aware of the possibility of 'disguised compliance' (Reder *et al*, 1993) which involves a parent or carer giving the appearance of co-operating with child welfare agencies to avoid raising suspicions, to allay professional concerns and ultimately to diffuse professional intervention. Examples include making small, but generally ineffective, changes which last only briefly; tidying up downstairs in time for a visit with upstairs remaining filthy; clearing away evidence of alcohol consumption; ensuring the male partner is

Response to change

		EFFORT	
		HIGH	**LOW**
COMMITMENT TO CHANGE	**HIGH**	Genuine commitment	Tokenism
	LOW	Compliance Imitation Approval seeking	Dissent Avoidance

(Howarth (2000) *The Child's World: Assessing children in need*, London and Philadelphia: Jessica Kingsley Publishers. Reproduced with kind permission of Jessica Kingsley Publishers)

out of the way when workers call; or making promises that aren't kept.

Ask workers from other agencies about parental co-operation. In this way, you can build up a picture of the extent of co-operation and identify where barriers exist. Always be aware that a low level of co-operation may mask continuing neglect of children.

The above grid, taken from Horwath (2001), may help in analysing levels of co-operation and can be used with Tony Morrison's (2006) adaptation of Prochaska and DiClemente's (1984) model of change (cited in Fauth and Shemmings, 2010). Morrison presents a series of sequential elements of motivation; it may be helpful to apply this in assessing levels of co-operation.

1. *I accept there is a problem*
2. *I have some responsibility for the problem*
3. *I have some discomfort about the impact, not only on myself, but also on my children*
4. *I believe things must change*
5. *I can be part of the solution*

6. *I can make choices about how I address the issues*
7. *I can see the first steps to making the change/can work with others to help me.*

(Fauth and Shemmings, 2010)

Look at co-operation/resistance at each stage of intervention and address, where possible, barriers to co-operation. Research tells us that outcomes are very poor for children where parents fail to recognise children's needs, are unable to take responsibility for maltreatment and dismiss the need for change (Fauth and Shemmings, 2010). When we think about parental resistance, we tend to focus on the parent–worker relationship and, of course, this is important. However, attending to the parent–child relationship will tell you more about parents' recognition and understanding of their child's needs and their commitment to the child and to change.

Focus on the child

It cannot be repeated too often that the focus must always remain on the child. When you visit a child's home, ask yourself: 'What is it like to be this child living in this family?' 'Was this child wanted and planned for?' The chronology of the child's life should contain information from conception if possible, a history of the child's caregivers, the quality of care the child received, changes of carers and significant moves and events in the child's life as well as periods of stability. Feeding into this will be information from other professionals involved in the child's care and those from adult services working with the parents. Your analysis should reflect knowledge of child development and any risks and threats to the meeting of developmental milestones. The input of health and education information will be critical in assessing all aspects of the child's development. Analysis should include identification of risk factors and opportunities for developing resilience (see below).

A focus on the child means a focus on the parent–child relationship. A significant feature of child neglect is the breakdown of the relationship of care.

Neglect involves a breakdown in relationship, which manifests as either an unwillingness or inability on the part of a child's primary carer to offer reliable and adequate care.

(Tanner and Turney, 2000, p 340)

In most cases the primary relationship is with the mother and this can lead to a general blaming of "bad mothers". This is not to exclude fathers' responsibility but, given that a number of fathers are absent or uninvolved in the care of the child, to understand the mechanisms at work the focus needs to be on the child's relationship with the primary caregiver. Tanner and Turney (2000) cite Crittenden's four levels of parental response.

1. *The parent must hear the child. For some parents, hearing the child is difficult amidst the overwhelming nature of their own needs and difficulties and the chaos of daily life.*
2. *The parent needs to interpret the child's response: this requires being attuned to the child's internal state and interpreting the child's need.*
3. *The parent needs to believe that they can take effective action. Many neglectful parents feel out of their depths and unable to act effectively.*
4. *The parent must respond effectively to the child.*

   (Crittenden, 1993)

The parent–child relationship can break down at any or all of these stages. Consider what the parent is thinking and feeling at each stage.

Tanner and Turney (2000) discuss Parker's concept of ambivalence (1995, 1997). Parenting is a developmental process and there are likely to be periods of maternal ambivalence or emotional unavailability. The important question is what leads to ambivalence or emotional unavailability becoming the defining characteristics of the relationship. To answer this question, you need to explore with the parent, again often the mother, her perceptions of herself, her role as a mother and how this affects her relationship with her child. This information, placed in the wider context of an ecological framework, can help you understand her parenting, especially when there is little effective partner or family support. Consider the nature and quality of the parent's personal and family relationships, the role of the informal and formal network in their lives as well as external factors such as the role of poverty, racism, domestic violence and maternal depression.

Consider also the parents' understanding of the reasons for their child's behaviour. One parent may attribute a small child crying to their distress and need for comfort. Another may see this behaviour as the child deliberately wanting to annoy them. It is not difficult to see which is the more dangerous. Understanding parents' perceptions of their children, the meaning they give to them and their behaviour is not always obvious, but through careful and documented observation, you may begin to understand the nature and subtle dynamics of the relationship (Tanner and Turney, 2000).

Focus on the needs of the disabled child

Kennedy and Wonnacott (2005) consider the assessment of developmental needs of the disabled child and caution against applying lower expectations of parenting simply because it is harder to meet the child's needs. There are a number of areas where the disabled child might be vulnerable to inadequate care. Feeding difficulties can result in a child being malnourished; sensory impairments can compromise the attachment process. The number of different carers involved, whether through the use of respite services or leaving a child with inappropriate babysitters, can expose the disabled child to risk of abuse and lack of stability and consistency of care. The disabled child is more vulnerable to teasing and bullying. The limited life expectancy as a result of some impairments may lead to the parent "distancing" themselves from the child, with consequences for bonding and attachment. Parents may have unrealistic (too high or too low) expectations of the child's achievements. They may lack interest in learning ways of communicating effectively with their child. They may either over-protect or fail to provide appropriate supervision and boundaries for their child.

Having a disabled child can affect the whole family. It is, therefore, essential to conduct a multi-agency assessment and ensure that the changing needs of the disabled child and the long-term nature of disability are acknowledged in the provision of services. You may need access to training on disability issues and communication. *Safeguarding Disabled Children: Practice guidance* (DCSF, 2009) includes information on useful resources for workers.

Assess parenting capacity

It is important for you to consider the *meaning* which parents attribute to parenting. A focus on the difficulties of parenting involves a shift away from focusing only on the legal responsibility to protect the child (what Woodcock (2003) calls the 'surface-static' notion of parenting) to understanding the underlying psychological factors associated with parenting. Instead of exhorting parents to change and then attributing a lack of change to "resistance", this approach focuses on what gets in the way of parenting effectively.

Reder *et al* (2003) present a framework for assessment that focuses on relationships (illustrated below). This addresses three main areas of relationships: the parent–child relationship, the child–parent relationship, and the family–context relationship. They are interested in interactional behaviour rather than the itemisation of individual

Revised framework for assessment of parenting

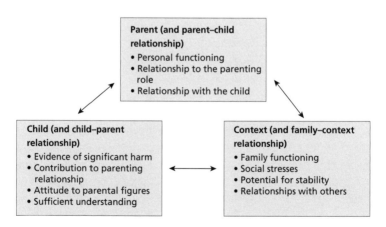

(Reder *et al* (eds) (2003) *Studies in the Assessment of Parenting*, London: Brunner-Routledge. Reproduced with kind permission of Brunner-Routledge)

factors. An example they give is in relation to parental youth. Being a young parent is a known risk factor, but it is more likely to be a significant factor in the light of their immature relationships with others in their life.

If we view child neglect as due fundamentally to a breakdown in care, then the assessment needs to focus on *the relationship of care*, particularly the parent's capacity for empathic care. Think about what evidence you have of the parent's ability to meet the child's needs in the context of 'empathic response to the level of harm experienced by their child' (Donald and Jureidini, 2004, p 8).

> *The quality of parenting is reflected in an adult's ability to recognise and adequately provide for, in a developmentally and emotionally appropriate manner, a child's current and anticipated needs. Adequate parenting is flexible enough to adapt to variability in those needs, and the particular child's repertoire of responsiveness, in the context of their social environment.*
>
> *(2004, p 8)*

Parents' capacity for empathy and sensitivity to their children's thinking and feeling will be influenced by their own childhood histories.

Assessment, therefore, should seek to understand the *interaction* between the developmental needs of the child, now and in the future, and the capacity of the parent to meet those needs within their particular environmental context. "Good enough parenting" means being able to be flexible and responsive. Although characteristics of the child (for example, age, disability, emotional disturbance) and of the environment (for example, poverty and access to supports) impinge on the quality of parenting, the child's experience of being parented is determined primarily by the parent (Donald and Jureidini, 2004).

Don't forget the role of fathers or father figures and their contribution to parenting, and be aware of some of the barriers to involving men.

These may be related to a number of factors: fathers' reluctance to be involved; cultural considerations surrounding the role of fathers; fear on the worker's part of a father's hostility; the very real risks faced when working with violent men; or the transitory nature of some men's involvement in family life. When father figures are not part of the assessment, you may fail to recognise the risk they present to the child or, alternatively, the contribution they could make to the child's life. At the same time, it is important to acknowledge that there are some violent and dangerous men whom it may be impossible to engage.

Consider parental lifestyle factors. Parental drug and alcohol misuse, domestic violence, mental illness and learning disability feature in the lives of many neglectful parents; these issues are addressed in greater detail in Tip 5. You will need to focus on the impact on the child of having, for example, a parent who misuses drugs or alcohol. Not all children are adversely affected, but some will be. Some children will have protective factors in their lives, for example, one parent who does not use alcohol or drugs, or a close family member who offers support and a refuge. How the parent manages their habit will indicate their ability to care for their child. Consider patterns of behaviour that emerge from social histories and chronologies: these provide information about past behaviour, impact of rehabilitation and relapses. Gather information from a variety of sources, both professional and informal. Use tools that can add to your assessment (for example, Dalzell and Sawyer's tool for assessing the impact of drug abuse on parenting capacity (2007, pp 80–81). Don't forget to ask the parents about their usage – how many units a day/week they drink; what drugs they use and how they are ingested; how alcohol/ drugs help them or cause problems for them; and their motivation to stop using.

The definition of significant harm includes 'impairment suffered from seeing or hearing the ill-treatment of another' (1.28, DCSF, 2010). Where domestic violence is a factor, children may live in a constant atmosphere of fear and dread. To what extent can the parent protect the child from this? What are the risks to the child of physical and emotional abuse? Can the parent, or anyone else, provide the child with a sense or place of safety and security?

Where the parent has a learning disability, consider the minimum level of skills, knowledge and parenting capability required to promote healthy development. Can the parent anticipate risk? Can they manage diverse and complex demands, for example, supervise the toddler climbing on the furniture at the same time as responding to the needs of a new baby? Can they be flexible in their thinking and responses to the changing needs of the child? Consider what level of support is appropriate and realistic to enable the learning disabled parent to meet their child's needs.

Practitioners should ensure that they have access to experts in the field of drug and alcohol misuse, domestic violence, mental illness and adult learning disability, and that they include the input of professionals from adult services in the assessment.

Consider the interaction of risk and resilience factors

To understand the impact of neglect, you need to consider signs in relation to the child's age and development, family and environmental factors, and agency response (Brandon *et al*, 2009). Obviously, infants are particularly vulnerable as they are physically fragile and depend totally for their survival on the care of others. Because the first three years of a child's life are so critical in terms of development, early disadvantage from unmet basic needs can have long-lasting effects. Pre-school children are mostly cared for within the home, and are at greater risk of being invisible to outside agencies and to becoming lost within a noisy, chaotic family environment where their needs go unheard and unattended to. They may depend on the alert health visitor, GP or early years practitioner to notice signs of neglect, particularly if the family is isolated and lacks a good support system.

Children in middle childhood spend several hours a day in school and this can serve as some protection from a neglectful home environment. For some children, school is a safe haven where they are heard and valued, but they may still be vulnerable at weekends and school holidays. Non-school attendance, evidence of chronic tiredness, hunger, poor health, and/or poor educational performance are all worrying signs and when put together may tell a story of significant neglect. Some of these children may be left to their own devices, witness domestic violence or have to care for younger siblings and parents under the influence of drugs or alcohol. School teachers, school nurses, activity group leaders as well as practitioners in adult mental health, domestic violence and substance misuse services are in a good position to pick up signs that all is not well.

The neglect of adolescents has, until recently, been a neglected topic (Stein *et al*, 2009, Hicks and Stein, 2010). Neglected adolescents form a very vulnerable group. These are young people who have often spent much of their childhood neglected and are, as a result, extremely troubled. Signs of neglect may include substance misuse, mental health difficulties, self-harm, anti-social or criminal behaviour, running away and a lack of willingness to engage with helping agencies. These young people may also be "lost" at home, with parents having either given up or lost interest in them. If the young person is still in school, non-school attendance, poor performance and behaviour difficulties are common. Some of them will be known to the police and youth offending teams. Presenting problems may be symptomatic of chronic neglect; a number of different services are likely to be in touch with some of these young people and should be alert to a possible history of neglect. Many of the adolescents who move from one placement to another in the care system are young people who have experienced chronic neglect.

The family environment, parents' own histories and their current lifestyle will all impact on the well-being of the child at different ages and stages of growing up. The way in which services respond to families can also constitute either protective or risk factors. If signs of concern have been noted but not acted upon, or where a concern may have been referred on but nobody has followed this up, a child may go unprotected. In some cases of neglect, a worry about being judgemental or culturally insensitive may prevent action. Likewise, if the child is allowed to get lost in the overwhelming and chaotic nature of the parents' difficulties, or the worker ends up feeling as hopeless and helpless as the parents themselves, the child can remain unprotected. When evaluating risk and protective factors in relation to child neglect, don't forget to consider agency response.

Examples of risk and protective factors

Risk	Protective
Child not seen ("lost")	Parent's positive attitude to pregnancy and birth
Chaotic, overwhelmed, hopeless nature of family	Parent's insight into own behaviour
Parental substance misuse, domestic violence, mental illness, learning disability	Child comes first Child has a secure base
Parent's history of poor parenting, being in care	Parent having experienced good parenting
No family support, isolated	Family support available
Multiple moves, different father figures	Accepts there is a problem
Low expectations of ability to change things	Motivated to change
Parental chronic self-harm	Health visitor, GP in contact with family and alert to signs of neglect
Refuses help, advice, keeps distance from services	
Child's non-school attendance	School staff alert to signs of neglect
Young person involved in anti-social/criminal behaviour	Police, youth offending services alert to signs of neglect
Young person's substance misuse, domestic violence	Mental health services alert to child neglect

Key protective factors for children include having a secure base (a good attachment relationship), self-esteem and self-efficacy. Authoritative parenting, which includes a balance of control and warmth, the provision of boundaries and attention to needs, and a close emotional bond between parent and child are strong protective factors.

Remember that some children can appear on the surface to be resilient. But we know that neglect undermines the very factors that lead to resilience. Don't mistake surviving for thriving. Understanding how the child functions, including the coping mechanisms they have developed, may reveal hidden trauma and stress.

Key points

- The assessment of the neglected child and their family should be within an ecological framework; analyse the interaction of the different dimensions within this framework.
- Plan the assessment; use theory and research to inform and develop ways of understanding.
- Consider using a range of tools to aid the assessment without the assessment becoming a checklist.
- Include the child's voice in the assessment. Ask yourself: 'What is it like to be this child in this family? What do I experience? How do I feel?'
- Ensure that you have the skills to communicate effectively with the child, the parents and other professionals.
- Analyse parental co-operation and resistance; assess motivation to change.
- Take a full social history. Use chronologies and genograms to understand patterns, family relationships, family functioning, risk and resilience factors.
- Consider neglect as the breakdown in the relationship of care; assess parenting capacity with this in mind. Focus on the parent's ability to provide empathic care.
- Consider the interaction of risk and resilience factors and the impact of parental lifestyle.
- In analysing the evidence, avoid the risks associated with accommodation, the rule of optimism and cultural relativism.

TIP 8

Recognise when children in public care are suffering neglect

Children and young people in care are entitled to expect to be safe and protected from harm. Unfortunately, however, some children experience maltreatment whilst in care or when placed for adoption. This tip considers how to identify neglect in foster care, residential care and adoptive placements and ways in which we can safeguard children and young people in care.

Learn the lessons from serious case reviews

We do not know the exact incidence of neglect of children and young people in care but there are some useful messages from serious case reviews. In the year ending 31 March 2009, of 173 serious case reviews, 17 were in relation to children in care or adopted from care (Ofsted, 2009). Of the 21 children concerned, 16 were aged 11 years or over. Although the Ofsted report does not identify particular instances of neglect, it does highlight significant shortcomings which will be relevant in cases of neglect.

Six groups of factors were identified as having contributed to deaths or serious incidents in children in public care:

1. *Insufficient focus by professionals on the needs of the children. Many of the children, particularly the older ones, had long and complex histories of concerns and episodes in care. The children's signs of unhappiness and cries for help were either not recognised or addressed insufficiently.*

2. *Shortcomings within the process for assessing the children and decision making. There was inconsistent quality in both assessment and decision making; sometimes a complex and confusing array of professionals involved, with disagreements about the care plan and appropriateness of the placement. There was also a delay in or lack of recognition of learning difficulties.*

3. *Lack of consistent rigour in the assessment and approval of foster carers and adopters. This included failing to give sufficient weight to their history; gaps in the assessment of family members; not taking the views of children or foster carers/adopters into account; and insufficient challenge by fostering or adoption panels. Sometimes the "rule of optimism" was applied; the significance of children's views was minimised; problems in placement denied because of the shortage of placements; and inappropriate assumptions made that carers could cope. There was also a failure to keep within the approval range of foster carers.*

4. *Failings in joint working between agencies. There was evidence of poor information sharing. Personal education plans were missing; accessing CAMHS was difficult; other agencies' responses were variable.*

5. *Lack of compliance with statutory requirements and guidance.* *There was evidence of poor lack of care plans, delays in notifying local authorities of placements, and placing children without introductions. Applying both child protection procedures and procedures for allegations against foster carers at the same time caused confusion.*

6. *Gaps in meeting staff training needs.* *Staff training needs included working with substance misuse, managing challenging behaviour, children who have been sexually abused and risk management.*

   (Ofsted, 2009)

Consider the characteristics of children and young people in public care

The care population constitutes some of the most vulnerable children in society, with ages ranging from birth to those on the cusp of adulthood. Each age group is vulnerable in different ways, from the newborn baby withdrawing from their mother's drugs or susceptible to Foetal Alcohol Effects, the young child with a history of neglect and abuse, the severely disabled child, to the disaffected teenager who has had numerous care placements and is now excluded from school. Common to all these is the experience of separation and loss and, in many cases, experience of abuse and/or neglect and damaged attachments.

For children, the separation from primary attachment figures can be traumatic. The sense of fear, abandonment and helplessness can be overwhelming. Young children, whose survival depends on their caregivers' ability to perceive and respond to need, experience heightened stress and fear when their needs go unmet. Children living in neglectful or abusive family environments can be in a constant state of anxiety and fear for their survival. High levels of stress hormones affect brain development and all areas of functioning. Children may have difficulty with speech and language and may be unable to express in words their powerful feelings. They have trouble with cognitive processes, making sense of their world, and an inability to empathise with others. Traumatised children have difficulty controlling their impulses and mood swings. Their short-term memory can be affected. They lack the capacity to enjoy the world around them. It is not uncommon for children to lack trust in adults, lack self-awareness, to have a poor sense of self and, in some, a tendency to dissociate.

Because many children in care have been traumatised, those caring for them need an appreciation of the impact of trauma on development and functioning, and an understanding of potential triggers to traumatic memories.

Recognise the signs of neglect of children and young people in care

The provision of care for children in foster care, residential care and adoption is governed by regulations and national minimum standards. The glossary to the Children's Homes National Minimum Standards for England and Wales describes neglect as:

> *Single or repeated failure to take appropriate action which results in harm or distress being suffered by the child or young person. Neglect can take many forms but includes the withholding of appropriate medicines, food and emotional support. It is characterised by the child or young person suffering from something not being done.*
>
> *(DH, 2002)*

It will also include the failure to promote healthy relationships (including attachments to foster carers or adoptive parents); to keep the child or young person safe from harm; to promote education, health and leisure pursuits; to help the child or young person develop independence skills; to promote contact with birth family and others in compliance with the care plan; and to promote a sense of identity.

For the child in care, there will be a number of people responsible for ensuring their needs are met, including the carer(s), the child's social worker and the carer's manager or supervisor. Neglect may occur either as a result of the failure of the carer to provide for the child's day-to-day needs or of the professionals involved to provide the services the child needs. Neglect can involve failure to comply with statutory requirements or policies and procedures where this impacts on meeting the child's needs.

We know that for some children the number of moves they experience can undermine their sense of security and stability and affect their capacity to make enduring relationships. Some are in placements unsuitable to their needs. Even for those with stable placements, there will be some who are unhappy with their arrangements. Failure to recognise and respond to signs of unhappiness can constitute neglect. Children and young people's cries for help might include behaviour designed to disrupt a placement, self-harm, running away and making allegations against carers. Careful matching of the child's needs and the capacities of the carer is vital, but just as important is for the child and carer to like each other.

If neglect is considered as the breakdown in the relationship of care, you need to focus not only on carers being able to meet the required standards of basic care but also on the quality of the relationship between carer and child, for example, evidence of emotional warmth in the relationship. If this is missing, carers can appear to "go through the motions" of caring but fail to engage with the child at an emotional level. Signs of emotional rejection include the child being treated differently from others in the household, being dressed shabbily, being expected to eat their meals in a different room from the carer's family and not being able to share in family events or celebrations. Emotional abuse can include expecting the child to meet the carer's unmet needs (for example, needs arising from infertility or an unhappy relationship) or having unrealistic or rigid expectations of the child. It can include making derogatory remarks about the child and their family.

Looking after damaged children is a complex and challenging task, and carers require a high level of knowledge and skill, tolerance and perseverance. Most children will respond well to sensitive, nurturing care and this is seen in the progress they make in different areas of their development. And, of course, lack of progress does not always indicate neglectful care: for some children who have been deeply damaged by earlier experiences, there may be little or no progress for long periods of time. Neglect should be considered in the context of the carer–child relationship. Consider the carer's capacity to be flexible in responding to the individual child's needs and to provide emotional warmth within a framework of security and protection.

Further examples of neglectful care might include not providing supervision appropriate to the child's needs or over-protecting the child through a fear of risk; being unwilling to attend school events or meetings; failing to provide the child with opportunities to make friends and develop their talents and interests; failing to promote contact with birth family; and not treating the child as a member of the foster/adoptive family.

Clarity of roles and responsibilities in the care team, the sharing of information and good communication between members will be crucial in identifying early signs of neglect. The adopted child and family may be in receipt of different post-adoption support services, and the same principles of information sharing will apply. Where there may be differences of opinion regarding the care plan, the quality of care the child is receiving or the assessment of the child and family's need for services, it is important that there is a senior manager with oversight of the case.

Ensure that recruitment and assessment processes aim to identify residential care workers, prospective foster carers and adoptive parents who can provide safe and secure care

Following the *Bichard Inquiry Report* (Bichard, 2005), the recruitment of people working with children is now more rigorous, with clearer processes for identifying those who are barred from working with children or vulnerable adults and a greater focus on risk assessment, statutory checks and references. However, no system is foolproof and we can never totally eradicate harm to children in care, but we can ensure that systems are as rigorous as possible. As the majority of looked after children are in foster and adoptive placements, this section focuses primarily on the assessment of foster carers and adopters; however, the skills and qualities required to provide safe and secure care in these contexts are also relevant to residential care.

Expectations of those in a caring role are high, hence the rigorous recruitment and approval process. The assessment of foster carers and adopters must be thorough, must focus on identifying strengths and vulnerabilities, and be well-evidenced and analytical. Assessment for safe carers will be supported by statutory checks and references and the verification of the information provided by the applicant. Adults who are secure and have a strong sense of identity and self-esteem are those best able to cope with the challenges of caring for children with emotional and behavioural difficulties. Walker identifies three key areas that the assessment should focus on:

- *The ability to manage a wide range of feelings, both in themselves and others;*
- *the resolution of any losses or traumas that they have experienced in their lives;*
- *the acquisition of reflective function.*

    (2008, p 49)

The ability to regulate and control emotions begins in infancy and early childhood and is dependent on early interactions with primary caregivers, hence the significance of exploring applicants' early childhood experiences and relationships. Carers must be in touch with and able to express and manage their own emotions in order to help children who may be overwhelmed by theirs. The resolution of earlier losses may be indicative of a carer's insight, their resilience and their sensitivity and understanding of the trauma and loss that a child may have suffered.

Reflective function is described as understanding the behaviour of oneself and others as being organised by thinking, feeling, beliefs, values and wishes (Fonagy and Target, 1997). This involves the ability to think flexibly about thoughts and feelings in oneself and others, sometimes known as "mind-mindedness". Being able to interpret the child's behaviour and understand the underlying need and motivation is particularly important when caring for a traumatised child. Reflective functioning involves having access to one's own defences. The capacity for reflective functioning makes it possible for the carer to help the child develop their own reflective capacity.

Those assessing prospective carers should also seek evidence of:

- a strong support network and the ability to seek and use support appropriately;
- an ability to manage difference and diversity – the ability to celebrate the uniqueness of each child;
- stability and commitment in relationships;
- an ability to resolve conflict;
- a capacity for openness and co-operation; and
- a child-centred approach.

If there are already children in the family, the assessment should include identifying individual strengths and vulnerabilities of the children and ensuring that each child has the opportunity to express their views about the family becoming a foster/adoptive family.

Where the assessment is of a family member or friend of the child, careful consideration should be given to their capacity to protect the child and maintain clear boundaries between their caring role and their role as a relative or friend of the child's parent. Where a child has been maltreated by their parent, attention should focus on the family culture, values and parenting patterns and the carer's ability to provide a better experience for the child. Take, for example, the child placed with their maternal grandmother. If the mother was herself neglected as a child, you will need to seek clear evidence of a significant change and improvement in parenting capacity before being satisfied that the placement will meet the needs of this child.

Undertake careful matching of the child with the carer or parent

National minimum standards for fostering and adoption emphasise the importance of careful matching of children's needs with carers' capacities. Residential care standards require that the child's needs fit with the designated purpose of the home. The matching process should consider the range of the child's developmental needs, their needs arising from their ethnicity, language, culture and religion and their views and wishes regarding the proposed placement. The capacity of the carers to meet these needs should be analysed carefully before decisions are made. Careful matching with a planned introductory period is more likely to occur in the case of long-term fostering or adoption, where child and carer have an opportunity to get to know each other before placement. The risks are higher for those placements, often short-term and emergency, where there is little opportunity for matching or for child and carer to establish a relationship (Sinclair *et al*, 2005).

No placement will be without some element of risk, making a risk assessment an important part of the matching process. Indicators of risk associated with the child will include background factors, a history of abuse and/or neglect, attachment difficulties and challenging behaviour. Indicators of risk associated with the adoptive parent/foster carer will include unresolved loss, unrealistic expectations of the child including the expectation of an early attachment, rigid thinking and inflexible parenting style. The probability of harm to the child will depend on the balance between predisposing factors in the carer, for example, how they manage stress, their sense of security or their confidence as new parents, their identified strengths, and the current situation, including the timeliness of the placement, and access to good support. A careful analysis of these different factors can help practitioners weigh the risks and benefits of the proposed placement and ensure that appropriate supports are in place.

Support the placement

The success of care placements depends on the capacity of carers to meet the needs of the child with the support of the care team. Support must be tailored to the individual needs of child and family/ carer; this might include, in some cases, procuring specialist therapeutic or counselling services. Those supporting carers should be sensitive to the emotional impact of children's difficulties on the carers and the risk of carers experiencing secondary traumatic stress. Early signs of secondary stress include tearfulness and anger, disruption of sleep and eating patterns, physical illness, irritability and withdrawing emotionally from the distress of the child. Practitioners may also notice that carers miss appointments, fail to seek support, fail to look after themselves properly, and increasingly feel isolated and unappreciated (Cairns and Fursland, 2007). Secondary traumatic stress can threaten the placement unless identified and addressed early on.

Foster carers and residential care workers need access to regular supervision, adoptive parents to good support, to enable them to meet the needs of children and young people. Regular supervision also provides another level of oversight of the care of the child and can alert managers to signs of neglect in the duty of care.

Statutory reviews should allow children and young people to express their views about their placement and their lives, but it can be very difficult for children to speak up about their unhappiness or dissatisfaction. Try to ensure that the child's voice is heard: spend time with the child; identify an advocate or another adult to support them; make sure they know how to make a complaint or have access to an appropriate helpline; identify and investigate changes in the child's behaviour or mood patterns. Avoid adopting a "rule of optimism" about the placement which may prevent you seeing signs of things going wrong.

> *Listen to us, check if we need anything, help us to stay in contact with our family, remember we are people.*
>
> *(Child quoted in Ofsted, 2010, p 22)*

Foster carers, careworkers and adoptive parents may need additional support in the form of specialist advice and consultation and respite care, and should have access to training and development opportunities.

Understand the responsibilities for safeguarding children in public care

Make sure that you are familiar with the statutory guidance on managing allegations and complaints against staff and carers who work with children in care. It is important to understand the different procedures and how they apply to individual cases. Where an allegation has been made and the decision of the local authority and the police is not to pursue a statutory child protection enquiry or police prosecution, the local authority Designated Officer will decide whether further action should be taken – disciplinary action in the case of a careworker, or investigation by an independent person with a view to review of approval in the case of a foster carer. In the case of an allegation being made against an adoptive parent before an adoption order has been granted, the same procedures will be followed as for foster carers. Once an adoption order has been made, the local authority will follow the same procedures as for any child living within their own family.

Further guidance on managing allegations against foster carers is available from *Managing Allegations and Serious Concerns about Foster Carers* (Fostering Network, 2006) and *Protecting Children – Supporting Foster Carers* (DCSF, 2006b).

Key points

- Ensure that the child's voice is heard. Be alert to signs of unhappiness or distress and cries for help.
- Rigorous recruitment and selection procedures and thorough evidence-based assessments of carers can minimise the risk of neglect of children in care.
- Many children in care have emotional and behavioural difficulties; looking after them can be very challenging and can have a significant impact on carers.
- Those in a caring role should have access to good support and supervision, with opportunities for further training and development.
- A focus on the relationship of care can help practitioners identify signs of neglect in care settings.
- To minimise the risk of children in care being neglected, ensure careful matching prior to placement and the provision of tailor-made support services.
- Following statutory and practice guidance on care placements can help ensure that children receive good quality care.
- Practitioners should be familiar with procedures for managing allegations against care workers and foster carers.
- Be aware of the possibility of agency neglect, which may take the form of not complying with the care plan, failing to notice signs of neglect, failing to listen to the child or failing to provide the services the child requires to meet their needs.

TIP 9

Use interventions effectively

> *I know what it is to feel abandoned and alone, worthless and unwanted. I knew these feelings long before I had words for them. It felt bad at the time and little has changed.*
>
> (Kevin Toni Mitchell, at age 18, quoted in Harris, 2008, p 62)

Intervention and child neglect

We know that, even with a sound knowledge and understanding of child neglect, knowing when and at what level to intervene can be challenging and difficult. Analyses of serious case reviews point to a lack of effective and timely intervention. Early signs of neglect are missed, together with an opportunity for early intervention that might prevent a situation escalating into something more serious and chronic. Identifying and responding to early signs depends on a level of knowledge and expertise that some of those delivering universal services or those for children with additional needs may not have. Intervention should occur when signs of vulnerability are apparent and not when it becomes evident that there is a risk of or actual significant harm. For practitioners and managers, this raises the issue of how thresholds operate and how limited resources are targeted effectively.

Unfortunately, there is little research on the effectiveness of interventions specifically for child neglect. Most of what is available addresses interventions with parents, with the evaluation of services for children largely neglected. However, Gardner's (2008) collaborative project helped identify some good practice pointers.

Basic good practice in neglect

- *Timely response to all expressions of concern about neglect*
- *An understanding of the child's day-to-day experiences*
- *Adequacy of child care must be addressed as the priority*
- *Engagement with mothers, fathers, male partners and extended family*
- *Clarity on parental responsibility and expectations*
- *Full assessment of the child's health and development*
- *Monitoring for patterns of neglect and change over time*
- *Avoiding assumptions and stereotypes*
- *Tracking families whose details change (name, address, school, GP, etc)*
- *Regular updates of records/communicating updates quickly and accurately*
- *Regular, systematic planning and review of outcomes and service effectiveness; including the views of children and family members*
- *Addressing underlying problems (poverty, isolation, violence, mental health, substance misuse) in a systematic way*
- *Regular, independent case audit*

  (Gardner, 2008, pp 70–71)

Understand the continuum of intervention and how this shapes responses to child neglect

Thresholds of need and intervention are generally understood in the context of four levels of intervention. For child neglect, this maps out as follows.

Level of need	Level of intervention
Level 1 – known risk factors may alert professionals to potential for neglect	Universal services for all children and families
Level 2 – signs of low level neglect, child and family with additional needs	Common Assessment Framework and Lead Professional
Level 3 – signs of neglect indicating child has complex needs	Children's social care threshold – "child in need", targeted family support services
Level 4 – signs of neglect indicating child at high risk	Child protection services, child protection plan, more focused and intensive intervention. Where child has suffered or is at risk of suffering significant harm, care proceedings, possible care placement

Most intervention in cases of child neglect is reactive. Where those working in universal services can identify risk factors or early signs of neglect, a more proactive response may be possible. Professionals from a range of services, from health and education to housing and youth services, may notice early signs of neglect which, if acted upon, might trigger a higher level of response. Midwives and health visitors have a valuable window of opportunity pre-birth and in the first weeks and months of a child's life to pick up difficulties in parenting and concerns for the child's welfare. Schools and youth services may be aware of low attendance, poor physical presentation, unhappiness, signs of self-harm, etc, in older children and young people. But universal services can't reach those who don't take up their services, and some families will avoid them. The neglected child is therefore not seen.

Where concerns are identified, universal services may be too generalist to make a difference and families will need more targeted services, which might range from specific parenting programmes, the input of an educational psychologist, specialist play services or targeted youth services. This will normally follow a Common Assessment Framework (CAF) assessment in England. Use of the CAF can begin to help identify patterns of behaviour and alert professionals to potential risk factors. Where it is identified that a child has more complex needs, a referral as a "child in need" will be made to children's social care services. At this point, an assessment using the *Framework for the Assessment of Children in Need and their Families* (DH, 2000a) or its equivalent will be undertaken. The lack of or a poor assessment can result in the failure to identify children as "children in need" at an early stage, and can lead to missed opportunities for effective earlier intervention. So it is worth considering an early referral and the benefits of a full assessment to reveal a more complete picture of the needs of the child and family.

When planning intervention, it is important to be clear about anticipated outcomes. Where these are not met within a timescale determined by the child's needs, you may need to reconsider the effectiveness of your intervention. Be prepared to question what you and others see; open up for discussion and debate signs and interpretations; and always be mindful of the risk of adopting a particular mindset in relation to an individual child or family. This can be particularly dangerous where the child is on the cusp between having additional and complex needs (levels 2 and 3), or between "child in need" and child protection services (levels 3 and 4). The case of Victoria Climbié is a case in point.

> *...a referral received by social services, which indicated the likelihood of non-accidental injuries to Victoria, was labelled from the outset as "a child in need". This framed all of that department's*

subsequent activities on the case, so that no child protection assessment was performed and professional efforts were mainly focused on finding the family suitable accommodation. Then, an earlier (mis-)diagnosis of scabies as the cause of her skin lesions was recurrently invoked to explain later signs of abuse. As information about the case was passed from one professional to another, it was repeatedly framed as "a child with scabies" rather than "a child who may have been physically abused". This considerably diluted the degree of urgency and perceived risk, while interventions were aimed at the wrong issues (housing instead of maltreatment).

(Reder and Duncan, 2004, p 104)

This is an example of how fixed thinking can blind professionals to signs of abuse. In some cases, it can determine the balance between supporting parental rights and self-determination and the statutory duty to protect the child.

Be proactive

It goes without saying that intervention must follow a full assessment so that it can be tailored to need. There is unlikely to be a single cause: neglect usually occurs as a result of an interaction of a range of factors. Because of this, no single intervention is likely to result in success. Families will respond more effectively to a mix of practical and therapeutic services delivered by a few key people who have established a relationship of trust with family members. Problem areas should be broken down, with focused intervention aimed at producing a clear and measurable change. Parents need workers who can engage with them actively and support them throughout the process of change in order for them to sustain motivation.

The timescale for change should always be with the child's developmental needs in mind. This means keeping the child's welfare at the centre of any programme of intervention and being aware of the potentially long-lasting impact of continuing poor parenting on the child's health and development. In some cases sufficient parental change may be unachievable or, in others, the process of change will be too slow with the risk of compromising the child's development. Where child and family intervention programmes are not successful, the child's needs must be the prime concern and care proceedings may need to be considered.

Working with resistant or reluctant parents means engaging with them as people first (Stevenson, 2007), taking an interest in their lives and their difficulties, acknowledging their personal histories, the social and economic struggles they face and issues arising from gender or ethnicity.

> *It's all about relationships. We are talking about dealing with people, with problems, with painful stuff. You have to know someone...trust them. They must be reliable and be there for you, if you are going to be able to talk about the things you don't want to. The things that scare you.*
>
> (A parent, Office of the Children's Commissioner, 2010)

Praise and encouragement can have a powerful effect on young parents who are rarely praised.

> *On one occasion I said, 'Well done, that was really good' about something little that she had done. She looked at me and her face lit up. 'No one has ever said well done to me before'. This was such an important step for this young mother.*
>
> (Family-nurse practitioner)

The Family-Nurse Partnership, an early intervention programme from the USA which has had some impressive results in reducing social exclusion in young people, is an intensive home visiting programme for selected women, their partners and infants. The programme is delivered from pregnancy to the child's second birthday by specially trained health visitors (Olds, 2006). Success is attributable, in part, to the relationship between the practitioner and the parents – one based on trust, continuity and intensive support. The practitioner–parent relationship needs to be a focus in working with neglect cases, where parents often start from a position of no trust in themselves or others to make a difference. The success of this particular type of intervention also demonstrates the advantage of long-term input.

There will be some parents whose resistance and antipathy will be hard to overcome. You need to be able to face them with a sense of confidence. You will need a sound knowledge of the history of the case and be very clear about the signs of neglect, know what you are going to say and always keep the child at the centre. The support of colleagues can be valuable as well as having an opportunity to rehearse what you need to say to the family.

Target intervention to the needs of the child and family

It may be difficult or impossible to change the behaviour of seriously dysfunctional families where there are signs of chronic neglect and, in these cases where intervention fails to make a difference to the child's life, care proceedings should be considered without delay. For other families, a range of interventions exist, evaluations of which suggest that some will make a difference in some cases (see Howe, 2005; Gardner, 2008; Thoburn et al, 2009).

For some families, where there are no imminent concerns about the child's welfare and where parents are amenable to support, providing targeted advice, information and guidance may help, together with access to family support services. For parents of children where difficulties in the parent–child relationship are at the heart of the problem, there are a range of parenting programmes and play skills training that involve teaching skills and encouraging parents to work together. These programmes are aimed at improving parents' confidence and communication and their active involvement with and enjoyment of their children. *The Incredible Years Parent Training Programme* is one example. The benefits of this programme, however, can be limited by external factors such as maternal depression, marital conflict, isolation and socio-economic pressures (Gardner, 2008). Intervention needs to be multi-faceted, including addressing problems associated with housing and benefits as well as working with adult services – mental health, domestic violence and drug and alcohol services.

Where there are more serious concerns about a child's development and health, problems at school, age-inappropriate behaviour, a breakdown in the parent–child relationship, social exclusion, concerns about parental lifestyle (domestic violence, substance misuse), parental mental illness or learning disability, interventions should be targeted to meet the specific needs of the child and family following a full assessment. Decisions about intervention should be based on an analysis of the particular needs of the child and family with an eye to research evidence of what works. Services might include Special Educational Needs services, youth offending team, specialist mental health or disability team, drug and alcohol services, family support services and specific parenting and play skills programmes.

Social work interventions are more likely to be effective when:

- problems are developing rather than entrenched;
- assessments are well-informed;
- interventions are based on logical reasoning as to why they should be effective for a particular child or family and are tailored to suit individual needs;
- there is an inter-agency response;
- a key worker provides consistency and continuity.

    (Walker, 2010)

Interventions directed at parents, such as cognitive behavioural approaches (MacDonald, 2005), can be effective but often need to be one of a range of interventions for families with multiple problems. Other interventions include multi-systemic family therapy and social network interventions, the latter focusing on improving social supports to isolated families.

Some of the early intervention programmes for parents with young children aim to increase the child's sense of secure attachment by focusing on improving the parent's sensitivity to the child's thinking and feeling, their involvement and responsiveness to the child (Howe, 2005).

> *Support and availability reduce parental stress. Less stressed carers invest more time and energy in their babies. Interventions that help parents become interested in what their babies might be thinking and feeling, and how thought and feeling affect behaviour, not only increase attachment security, but also promote healthy psychosocial development and improve children's ability to self-regulate.*
>
> *(Howe, 2005, p 233)*

For older children and young people, Cognitive Behaviour Therapy and Multi-Systemic Therapy are specific interventions that may have a place alongside a multi-faceted approach to reduce family problems, including involving school, health, youth offending services, etc, and initiatives to build resilience.

Building resilience – factors that promote resilience

- A secure attachment to one or both parents
- A sense of self-esteem and self-efficacy
- Sociability
- Relationships with other supportive adults
- A supportive friendship network
- Regular attendance and continuity of schooling
- Opportunities for problem-solving
- Opportunities to develop hobbies and talents

Many of the services available focus on parents and younger children (Farmer and Lutman, 2010). But older children and their parents also need targeted support, particularly where those children have experienced lengthy periods of poor parenting with the consequent effects on their behavioural and emotional well-being.

A sound knowledge of attachment theory and child development, together with an evidence base for intervention, will help in planning work with the family and evaluating outcomes.

Provide a caring environment for children and young people unable to remain at home

Where the health and development of the child is seriously compromised by living in a neglectful environment and/or where attempts to improve parenting capacity have failed, a care placement is likely to be the best way to safeguard and promote the child's welfare.

Social workers must consider placement with a family member or friend before looking at other alternatives, and in some cases this will be appropriate. A thorough assessment of their capacity to care for the child is essential. Consider the family/kinship culture: is the child's experience of neglect part of a wider family culture of neglect? Are there intergenerational patterns of poor parenting, childhood abuse or neglect, substance misuse, domestic violence? Can this family member provide the child with the care, protection and nurturing they need? It is important to balance the vulnerability of the child and the extent of their unmet needs with the capacity of the proposed carer to provide the kind of environment and level of care the child will require. You may be failing the child, and risking disruption of the placement, if the carer is not up to the task.

Children who have suffered chronic neglect will need care that, first and foremost, provides them with a sense of safety and security. Schofield and Beek's (2006) secure base framework is an attachment-related model that promotes attachment through five key components of care.

Some children may need additional therapeutic input. There are a range of attachment-related therapies available, although the evidence base for their effectiveness is poor. Some of them are long-term and intensive. They mainly focus on promoting the child's attachment to their carer. For a fuller description of attachment-related interventions, see Part V of David Howe's book, *Child Abuse and Neglect: Attachment, development and intervention* (2005).

Social workers should seek a placement with foster carers (or adoptive parents) who are attuned to children's needs and can respond sensitively and empathically, using the components of this framework. For older children and young people accommodated in residential care, this framework can be applied both individually to the care of the young person and to the care home itself to ensure that the overall environment provides a sense of safety and security for its residents.

Carers will need full information about the child, including the family history, the child's history and their relationships, so that they have some sense of the child's capacity to respond to re-parenting. The assessment of the child should reveal how they see themselves and others – their sense of self-esteem, whether they view adults as able to provide safety and a secure base from which to explore, play and learn. Carers will need information about the child's understanding and ability to manage and express a range of feelings (oppositional and aggressive or withdrawn behaviour may indicate a failure to manage feelings appropriately). Observation of the child with their parents can tell you a lot about their behaviour, feelings and sense of self-esteem. Does the child feel helpless and incompetent in the presence of others or do they have a need to control those around them? What does being part of a family mean to the child? In some cases family is a cold, loveless and frightening idea. The challenge to carers is to help the child see family membership as providing safety and security and a place from which to grow and blossom.

Key points

Effective intervention depends on:

- a comprehensive assessment of the child and family;
- multi-faceted approaches to address the range of complex difficulties;
- being prepared to engage in long-term intervention;
- being prepared for early and later interventions, both in terms of the timing of intervention and the age of the child or young person;

- taking evidence-based decisions on interventions that can make a difference;
- considering protective as well as risk factors, and including interventions that build resilience;
- ensuring that intervention is parent-friendly;
- involving father figures as well as mothers;
- including attachment-focused interventions.

TIP 10

Know when enough is enough

One of the most difficult things for those working with neglected children and their families is knowing when enough is enough: in other words, when legal action should be taken and the child removed from their parents' care. Our legal definitions are open to interpretation. The DCSF (2010) definition of neglect refers to the 'persistent failure' to meet a child's needs – how do we interpret this in relation to ongoing neglect? What does 'adequate' mean in relation to the provision of basic needs and supervision? Thresholds for intervention vary; sometimes seem high and our expectations of "good enough" parenting low.

This tip considers the kind of evidence that can help you reach decisions about those cases where enough is enough.

Consider "significant harm" in relation to child neglect

Children Act 1989 (England and Wales) Significant harm – threshold criteria

A court may make a care order or supervision order in respect of a child if it is satisfied that:

● the child is suffering, or is likely to suffer, significant harm; and
● the harm, or likelihood of harm, is attributable to a lack of adequate parental care or control (s31 Children Act 1989)

Where the question of whether harm suffered by a child is significant turns on the child's health and development, his health or development shall be compared with that which could reasonably be expected of a similar child.

(s31(10) Children Act 1989)

In England and Wales legislation, for instance, the focus is on the impact of significant harm being attributable to inadequate parental care or control. Our understanding of what is adequate care hinges on what we would expect of a reasonable parent. Where there are financial and material difficulties, an early assessment should identify the impact of these difficulties and a support plan can be put in place to address them. Evidence should be gathered on an ongoing basis of the effectiveness of this support. The failure to effect changes in parenting behaviour and the failure to identify improvements in the child's health and development will raise further questions as to the cause.

In relation to the disabled parent or the parent with learning difficulties, how do we define 'adequate parental care or control'? This needs to be considered in relation to the impact of parenting on the child's health and development and what could 'reasonably be expected of a similar child'. The focus should always be on the child's welfare. If targeted and appropriate support to the parent has failed to make a difference, you may need to consider alternative care for the child. Parental motivation will be a key consideration in any assessment but the inability to make changes will be the deciding factor. Changes in parental behaviour must be related to changes in the child's health and development.

> *What are the indispensable, minimally adequate types of care that children require? What actions or failures to act on the part of the parents constitutes neglectful behaviour? What is the relevance of the parents' state of mind – does their neglect have to be wilful or not?*
>
> *(Iwaniec et al, 2004, p 427)*

One of the difficulties in applying definitions is that parental care or lack of it will impact on different children in different ways. The impact of poor care will have a more serious and faster effect on the younger and/or disabled child than on others (Dickens, 2007). Individual differences in the child's character and temperament can sometimes make it harder to parent some children. Ultimately, the question of whether enough is enough will hinge on whether parents are able to provide care that is, at least, 'minimally adequate' (Iwaniec *et al*, 2004). 'Minimally adequate' care must ensure that the child's health and development is what you would reasonably expect of a similar child.

In cases of neglect, the emphasis on harm and its effect on health and development means that 'there does not have to be a decisive event to satisfy the grounds, rather clear evidence of any harm that the child is suffering, or likely to suffer if the order were not made' (Dickens, 2007, p 78). However, it is sometimes easier to evidence significant harm in relation to an event of abuse. That is why it is more likely for one event of physical or sexual abuse to "catapult" a case into care proceedings than ongoing neglect (Dickens, 2007).

Referring to the removal of children at an interim stage, the Court of Appeal, in *Re L-A [2009] EWCA (Civ) 822*, confirmed that children do not have to be at imminent risk of really serious harm to trigger removal from home, but there must be evidence that the children's safety requires interim protection. Therefore you will need to be able to account for why action is being taken now. There are two key questions when going into care proceedings. What are the likely long-term effects of neglect on the child, and do they justify an alternative permanence plan? And, is neglect having a significant impact on the child now, meaning that the child can no longer be left in the family home? Your legal adviser will want to know what difference it will make, if a child has been left in a negative environment for some time, to leave them there longer; whether removal at the beginning of proceedings is a proportionate response to the harm being suffered; and whether removal at this stage will pre-judge the eventual outcome. These are difficult issues, requiring clear evidence and a focus on the child's welfare now and in the future for resolution.

Evidence of the need for action will be strengthened by comprehensive chronologies that identify single episodes and ongoing neglect as well as providing an overview of events, evidence of intervention and its impact, and the cumulative effect of parental care on the child's health and development. Episodes of compliance or slight improvement have to be seen in the context of the overall picture. Is there a significant improvement in the care of the child or is this case one of ups and downs with a downward trend, or a case of chronic neglect "bumping along the ground"?

We tend to work from the default position that it is best for the child to be cared for within their own family, and our efforts are geared towards making that happen. It is important to question this assumption – it is clearly not best for some children to remain at home. There is a risk that this mindset encourages more and more attempts to keep the child at home in the face of evidence, often at an early stage, that this will not work.

Ward *et al*'s (2010) study shows the risk to development and behaviour when there is a delay in decision-making whilst professionals wait for parents to make the necessary changes. In their study there was an 'almost universal expectation' that children would remain with their parents, and decision-making appeared to be based on parental rights and empowerment rather than on children's needs.

Have early discussions with your legal adviser

Local authority social workers should speak to their legal advisers at an early stage in neglect cases. Where there is a child protection plan there should be close monitoring of the child. We know from research, however, that some children continue to be neglected. Farmer and Lutman (2010) found that two-fifths of the children in their research cohort were not adequately safeguarded, even with child protection plans, and that 28 per cent of the children were left with their parents in adverse circumstances before care proceedings were initiated. With a proactive approach to care planning from the start, children will hopefully be better safeguarded. Where children remain at home for long periods before care proceedings are finally initiated, they will need robust monitoring to ensure they do not suffer further maltreatment. Where a decision is made to remove them from a child protection plan and return them to "child in need" status, close monitoring should continue to ensure that a further deterioration does not occur.

In some cases, the threat of care proceedings may actually act as a motivator to parents to change (Iwaniec *et al*, 2004). But motivation has to be maintained over time to make a significant difference to the child.

Bring together the evidence supporting the need for legal intervention

You must be able to provide evidence of harm from neglect and unreasonable parenting. Standards of care may have fluctuated over time but it is the big picture that counts. Where there has been failure to progress the child protection plan, and where evidence points to lack of parental co-operation, deliberate non-compliance or inability to make the required changes in the required timescale, legal action may well be warranted. You must be prepared to challenge parents and confront them with non-compliance, or false compliance through minimal co-operation.

One of the difficulties in evidencing neglect is where there appear to be signs of neglect in one area of care but not in others. It is important to ask yourself what this could mean, and to consider the extent to which this area of neglect impacts on and interacts with other aspects of functioning. When someone tells you that the child whose physical needs are neglected has a strong bond with their parent, this merits careful investigation. Physical neglect has emotional consequences. A parent who persistently fails to provide sufficient food, clothing, warmth or supervision for a child is also denying the child the sense of security and safety they need from their caregiver. A strong emotional bond between parent and child suggests a parent who is attuned to their child's physical and mental state, understands what the child needs and is able to respond appropriately.

Describing a child as having a "strong" bond with a parent is unhelpful. The quality of the attachment is more important than the strength of it. We know that children can have strong ties to their parents that are based on a deep sense of insecurity and fear of abandonment. Describe and analyse the attachment behaviour to help you understand the nature of the attachment. The child who experiences neglect but is also described as having a strong bond with a parent may be a very insecure and frightened child.

The gathering and presentation of evidence relies on complete and up-to-date recording. Good recording:

- includes telephone and face to face contacts;
- is contemporaneous;
- includes a chronology and genogram;
- is concise and factual;
- includes observation;
- records parental attitudes;
- records failures to attend appointments;
- records evidence of non-compliance;
- includes a plan of action;
- includes the child's voice (wishes and feelings).

Evidence for neglect should consider the following:

- A genogram of the family
  This can identify inter- and intra-generational patterns of neglect in the family, including identifying the history and whereabouts of siblings. If older children in the family have been neglected and are now in substitute care, this history should be analysed in relation

to change/lack of change in the parents' situation and parenting capacity.

● A chronology
This will help identify single events over time but also provide a picture of the cumulative effects of neglect. Single events of neglect, episodes of ongoing neglect can be analysed in relation to the impact on the child's development (with particular focus on the interaction of neglect and sensitive periods of development). A chronology can demonstrate fluctuations of care with an analysis of the emerging patterns, for example, its persistent nature. Interpretations that are based on the sharing of information should be shared with other professionals to provide a clearer and fuller picture.

● Developmental charts and other monitoring measures
Clear and regular monitoring, including the use of height and weight charts, provide evidence of the child's progress. Records from adult services, for example, drug and alcohol services, may give further evidence of lack of change in parental behaviour.

● What the child says
This needs to be in the context of age and development and their capacity to express wishes and feelings. Observation of children with their parents and in different contexts can provide useful evidence. In some cases, children will not be freed up to speak until they are removed from their parents and in a safe place.

● The likelihood of change
  • The chronology and parental and family history can provide evidence of parental motivation and capacity to change. Guard against over-optimism. Judgements about capacity to change need to be measured against the child's timescale.
  • Don't make judgements on early impressions and information only – your judgement should be based on continual re-evaluation of evidence as it emerges.
  • Evidence from all the different services involved with the family makes up the big picture.
  • Back up evidence with research. For example, research suggests that for very young children with mothers who have

entrenched drug and alcohol problems, successful reunification within the child's timescale is very unlikely (Ward *et al*, 2006).

- The child's timescale
  - Young children cannot wait for parents to change. The environment children live in during their first three years can affect their long-term growth and development. Timescales for older children are important too – all children need security and stability and interested caregivers. Evidence can include the impact of parental behaviour on developmental delay and evidence of the difficulty for "catch up" in some areas of development.
  - Analysis of the lack of effectiveness of intervention in changing the child's life and the potential impact of further delay in taking action add to the urgency of the situation.

- Analysis of risk and resilience factors
  - Weigh up the risks to the child's health and development with signs of strength in the child and family. Remember that neglect undermines the key components of resilience – a secure base, good self-esteem and a sense of self-efficacy.
  - Have a clear, agreed understanding of thresholds and "good enough" parenting; analyse evidence of neglect against these.

Use a reliable evidence base as the foundation for decision-making. Consider the factors associated with predictions of future harm; refer to the chapter by Jones *et al* in *The Developing World of the Child* (Aldgate *et al*, 2006)

Consider the child's permanence needs

All children require a sense of permanence and stability in their lives. This includes:

- a positive feeling of belonging in a family, and of being loved and valued both for themselves and as a member of the family;
- a sense of security, predictability and stability in their lives;
- a positive sense of identity;
- feeling part of an extended family and wider network of friends;

● developing independence skills so that they can cope with the wider world – this includes education, employment, maintaining adult relationships, becoming an independent adult.

Ask yourself to what extent the child's family life can provide for these needs. What will be the impact on the child in later years if they fail to achieve a sense of permanence, stability and belonging? For children who need care outside the birth family, outcomes in terms of permanence and stability are age-related: the younger the child at placement, the better the outcome. The longer you delay in taking action, the greater the risk to achieving permanence for the child.

Key points

● Be clear about thresholds for legal intervention. Consult with professional colleagues and your legal adviser from an early stage.

● Agree with other professionals involved with the family on what you consider to be acceptable levels of parenting. Ensure your thresholds are not too high or your expectations too low.

● Ensure that you are knowledgeable about child development, attachment and the impact of neglect on children's well-being and life chances.

● Consider parental behaviour in relation to the impact on the health and development of the child.

● Legal action in neglect cases does not have to depend on a decisive event; chronic neglect is ongoing and the damage cumulative. Beware of allowing neglect to continue. Consider the need for urgent action.

● Gather evidence in a robust way from the start. This will include chronologies and clear and concise recording. Discuss interpretation of evidence with other professionals.

● Work to the child's timescale and keep the child's welfare central to your deliberations and actions. Delay, particularly for young children, can have damaging consequences in the long term. Consider the child's need for permanence and stability.

● Ensure that assessments are not purely descriptive but include good analysis.

Afterword

Throughout this book, there have been references to the complex nature of child neglect and the difficulties for practitioners working with families where neglect is an issue. There are no simple solutions that a Ten Top Tips publication can provide. But there are some strong messages.

- Never lose sight of the child.
- Work within the child's timescale: don't allow delay to compromise the child's well-being.
- Listen to the child – even the pre-verbal child can "talk" to you through their behaviour, their physical and emotional presentation.
- Be prepared to question, confront and challenge poor standards of care and poor standards of professional practice.
- Child neglect is not a nebulous, value-laden concept; it is possible to gather robust evidence of neglect.

The true measure of our professional practice lies in the future of the children we work with, and their future depends on us applying the same high expectations and standards of care that we would apply to children in our own families.

Bibliography

Bichard M (2005) *The Bichard Inquiry Report*, London: The Stationery Office

Bion WR (1962) *Learning from Experience*, London: William Heinemann

Brandon M, Belderson P, Warren C, Howe D, Gardner R, Dodsworth J and Black J (2008) *Analysing Child Deaths and Serious Injury through Abuse and Neglect: What can we learn? A biennial analysis of serious case reviews, 2003–2005*, London: DCSF

Brandon M, Bailey S, Belderson P, Gardner R, Sidebotham P, Dodsworth J, Warren C and Black J (2009) *Understanding Serious Case Reviews and their Impact: A biennial review of serious case reviews, 2005–2007*, London: DCSF

Burton S (2009) *The Oversight and Review of Cases in the Light of Changing Circumstances and New Information: How do people respond to new (and challenging) information?*, C4EO Safeguarding: briefing 3, available at: www.c4eo.org.uk/themes/safeguarding/files/safeguarding_briefing_3.pdf

Cairns K and Fursland E (2007) *Trauma and Recovery*, London: BAAF

Calder MC and Hackett S (eds) (2003) *Assessment in Childcare: Using and developing frameworks for practice*, London: Russell House Publishing

Child Welfare Information Gateway (2001) *Understanding the Effects of Maltreatment on Early Brain Development*, London: CWIG, available at: www.childwelfare.gov/

Cooper C (1985) '"Good enough", borderline and "bad enough" parenting', in Adcock M and White R (eds) *Good Enough Parenting*, London: BAAF

Corrigan M and Moore J (2011) *Communicating with Vulnerable Children*, London: BAAF

Crittenden P (1993) 'An information processing perspective on the behaviour of neglectful parents', *Criminal Justice and Behaviour*, 20:1, pp 27–48

Crittenden P (1999) 'Child neglect: causes and contributors', in Dubowitz H (ed) *Neglected Children: Research, practice and policy*, Thousand Oaks, CA: Sage

Dalzell R and Sawyer E (2007) *Putting Analysis into Assessment: Undertaking assessments of need*, London: NCB

Department for Children, Schools and Families (2003) *Every Child Matters*, London: DCSF

Department for Children, Schools and Families (2006a) *What to do if you're Worried a Child is Being Abused?*, London: The Stationery Office

Department for Children, Schools and Families (2006b) *Protecting Children – Supporting Foster Carers*, London: DCSF

Department for Children, Schools and Families (2009) *Safeguarding Disabled Children: Practice guidance*, London: DCSF

Department for Children, Schools and Families (2010) *Working Together to Safeguard Children*, London: DCSF

Department for Education (2010a) *Haringey Local Safeguarding Children Board Serious Case Review 'Child A'*, London: DfE

Department for Education (2010b) *Children In Need in England, including their Characteristics and Further Information on Children who were the Subject of a Child Protection Plan (2009–10 Children in Need census, Final)*, London: DfE, available at: www.education.gov.uk/rsgateway/DB/STR/d000970/index.shtml

Department for Education and Skills (2002) *National Minimum Standards for Fostering Services*, London: DfES

Department for Education and Skills (2005) *National Minimum Standards for Adoption Services*, London: DfES

Department for Education and Skills (2006) *Protecting Children – Supporting Foster Carers*, London: DfES

Department of Health (2000a) *Framework for the Assessment of Children in Need and their Families*, London: The Stationery Office

Department of Health (2000b) *Assessing Children in Need and their Families: Practice guidance*, London: The Stationery Office

Department of Health (2002) *Children's Homes National Minimum Standards for England & Wales*, London: DH

Dickens J (2007) 'Child neglect and the law: catapults, thresholds and delay', *Child Abuse Review*, 16, pp 77–92

Dingwall R, Eekalaar J and Murray T (1995) *The Protection of Children: State intervention and family life*, Oxford: Blackwell

Donald T and Jureidini J (2004) 'Parenting capacity', *Child Abuse Review*, 13, pp 5–17

Egeland B and Sroufe A (1981) 'Developmental sequelae of maltreatment in infancy', in Rizley R and Cicchetti D (eds) *New Directions for Child Development*, San Francisco, CA: Jossey Bass

Egeland B, Sroufe A and Erikson M (1983) 'The developmental consequences of different patterns of maltreatment', *Child Abuse and Neglect*, 7, pp 459–69

Fahlberg V (1994) *A Child's Journey through Placement*, London: BAAF

Farmer E and Lutman E (2010) *Case Management and Outcomes for Neglected Children Returned to their Parents: A five year follow up study*, DCSF-RB214, London: DCSF

Fauth R and Shemmings D (2010) *Effective practice to protect children living in "highly resistant" families*, C4EO Safeguarding Knowledge Review 1, London: C4EO

Ferguson H (2009) 'Performing child protection: home visiting, movement and the struggle to reach the abused child', *Child and Family Social Work*, 14, pp 471–480

Fonagy P and Target M (1997) 'Attachment and reflective function: their role in self-organisation', *Development and Psychopathology*, 9, pp 679–700

Forrester D, McCambridge J, Waissbein C, Emlyn-Jones R and Rollnick S (2006) 'Child risk and parental resistance: can motivational interviewing improve the practice of child and family social workers in working with parental alcohol misuse?' *British Journal of Social Work*, 38:7, pp 1302–1319

Fostering Network (2006) *Managing Allegations and Serious Concerns about Foster Carers*, London: Fostering Network

Gardner R (2008) *Developing an Effective Response to Neglect and Emotional Harm to Children*, Norwich and London: UEA and NSPCC, available at: www.nspcc.org.uk/inform

Gaudin J 1993) *Child Neglect: A guide for intervention*, Washington DC: National Center on Child Abuse and Neglect (US Department of Health and Human Services)

Glaser D and Prior V (1997) 'Is the term child protection applicable to emotional abuse?', *Child Abuse Review*, 6:5, pp 315–329

Harris P (ed) (2008) *The Colours in Me: Writing and poetry by adopted children and young people*, London: BAAF

Helm D (2010) 'Making sense of child and family assessment: how to interpret children's needs', London: Jessica Kingsley Publishers

Hicks L and Stein M (2010) *Neglect Matters: A multi-agency guide for professionals working together on behalf of teenagers*, London: DCSF

HM Government (2009) *Safeguarding the Disabled Child: Practice guidance*, London: DCSF

HM Government (2010) *Working Together to Safeguard Children: A guide to inter-agency working to safeguard and promote the welfare of children*, London: DCSF

Holland S (2004) *Child and Family Assessment in Social Work Practice*, Thousand Oaks, CA: Sage

Horwath J (ed) (2001) *The Child's World*, London: Jessica Kingsley Publishers

Horwath J (2002) 'Maintaining a focus on the child? First impressions of the Framework for the Assessment of Children in Need and their Families in cases of child neglect', *Child Abuse Review*, 11:4, pp 195–213

Horwath J (2005) 'Is this child neglect: the influence of differences in perceptions of child neglect on social work practice', in Taylor J and Daniel B (eds) *Child Neglect: Practice issues for health and social care*, London: Jessica Kingsley Publishers

Horwath J (2007a) 'The missing assessment domain: personal, professional and organisational factors influencing professional judgements when identifying and referring child neglect', *British Journal of Social Work*, 37:8, pp 1285–1303

Horwath J (2007b) *Child Neglect: Identification and assessment*, Basingstoke: Palgrave Macmillan

House of Commons Health Committee (2003) *The Victoria Climbié Inquiry Report*, London: TSO

Howe D (2005) *Child Abuse and Neglect: Attachment, development and intervention,* Basingstoke, Palgrave Macmillan

Hughes D (2006) *Building the Bonds of Attachment: Awakening love in deeply troubled children*, Northvale, NJ: Jason Aronson

Iwaniec D, Donaldson T and Allweis M (2004) 'The plight of neglected children: social work and judicial decision-making, and management of neglect cases', *Child and Family Law Quarterly*, 16:4, pp 423–436

Jones D, Hindley N and Ramchandani P (2006) 'Making plans: assessment, intervention and evaluating outcomes', in Aldgate J, Jones D, Rose W and Jeffery C (eds) *The Developing World of the Child*, London: Jessica Kingsley Publications

Jowitt S (2003) *Child Neglect: Contemporary themes and issues: policy and practice in child welfare*, Literature Review series 2, Glasbury-on-Wye: Bridge Publishing House

Kennedy M and Wonnacott J (2005) 'Neglect of disabled children', in Taylor J and Daniel B, (eds) *Child Neglect: Practice issues for health and social care*, London: Jessica Kingsley Publishers

Laming H (2003) *The Victoria Climbié Inquiry Report* (Cm 5730), London: The Stationery Office

MacDonald G (2005) 'Intervening with neglect', in Taylor J and Daniel B (eds) *Child Neglect: Practice issues for health and social care*, London: Jessica Kingsley Publishers

McCracken DG (1988) *The Long Interview*, Beverly Hills, CA: Sage

McLeod A (2008) *Listening to Children: A practitioner's guide*, London: Jessica Kingsley Publishers

Ministry of Justice (2008) *The Public Law Outline*, London: Ministry of Justice

Minty B and Pattinson G (1994) 'The nature of child neglect', *British Journal of Social Work*, 24:6, pp 733–48

Moran P (2009) *Neglect: Research evidence to inform practice*, London: Action for Children

Morrison T (2006) *Staff Supervision in Social Care: Making a real difference for staff and service users* (3rd edition), Brighton: Pavilion

NICE (2009) When *to Suspect Child Maltreatment, Clinical Guidelines CG89*, July 2009, revised December 2009, London: NICE

Office of the Children's Commissioner (2010) *Family Perspectives on Safeguarding and on Relationships with Children's Services*, London: Office of the Children's Commissioner

Ofsted (2009) *Learning Lessons from Serious Case Reviews*, London: Ofsted

Ofsted (2010) *Children's Messages on Care: Report by Children's Rights Director for England*, London: Ofsted

Olds DL (2006) 'The nurse-family partnership: an evidence-based preventive intervention', *Infant Mental Health Journal*, 27:1, pp 5–25

Parker R (1995) *Torn in Two: The experiences of maternal ambivalence*, London: Virago

Parker R (1997) 'The production and purposes of maternal ambivalence', in Hollway W and Featherstone B (eds) *Mothering and Ambivalence*, London: Routledge

Parrott B, MacIver A and Thoburn J (2007) *Independent Inquiry Report into the Circumstances of Child Sexual Abuse by Two Foster Carers in Wakefield*, Wakefield: Wakefield MBC

Perry BD (2002) 'Childhood experience and the expression of genetic potential: what childhood neglect tells us about nature and nurture', *Brain and Mind*, 3, pp 79–100

Prochaska JO and DiClemente CC (1984) *The Transtheoretical Approach: Crossing traditional boundaries of therapy*, Homewood, IL: Dow Jones-Irwin

Reder P and Duncan S (1999) *Lost Innocents: A follow-up study of fatal child abuse*, London: Brunner-Routledge

Reder P and Duncan S (2004) 'From Colwell to Climbié: inquiring into fatal child abuse', in Stanley N and Manthorpe J (eds) *The Age of Inquiry: Learning and blaming in health and social care*, London: Routledge

Reder P, Duncan S and Lucey C (eds) (2003) *Studies in the Assessment of Parenting*, London: Brunner-Routledge

Reder P, Duncan S and Gray M (1993) *Beyond Blame: Child abuse tragedies revisited*, London: Routledge

Rose W and Barnes J (2008) *Improving Safeguarding Practice: Study of serious case reviews 2001–2003*, London: DCSF

Ruch G (2007) 'Reflective practice in contemporary child-care social work: the role of containment', *British Journal of Social Work*, 37:4, pp 659–68

Rutter M, Beckett C, Castle J, Kreppner J, Stevens S and Sonuga-Barke E (2009) *Policy and Practice Implications from the English and Romanian Adoptees (ERA) Study: Forty five key questions*, London: BAAF

Schofield G (1998) 'Making sense of the ascertainable wishes and feelings of insecurely attached children', *Child and Family Law Quarterly*, 10:4, pp 363–376

Schofield G and Beek M (2006) *Attachment Handbook for Foster Care and Adoption*, London: BAAF

Scottish Executive (2004) *Scotland's Children's Charter*, Edinburgh: Scottish Executive

Sidebotham P (2007) 'Fatal child maltreatment', in Sidebotham P and Fleming P (eds) *Unexpected Death in Childhood*, Chichester: Wiley

Sinclair I, Wilson K and Gibbs I (2005) *Foster Placements: Why they succeed and why they fail*, London: Jessica Kingsley Publishers

Spencer N and Baldwin N (2005) 'Economic, cultural and social contexts of neglect', in Taylor D and Daniel B (eds) *Child Neglect: Practice issues for health and social care*, London: Jessica Kingsley Publishers

Srivastava O, Fountain R, Ayre P and Stewart J (2003) 'The Graded Care Profile' in Calder M and Hackett S (eds) *Assessment in Child Care: Using and developing frameworks for practice*, London: Russell House Publishing

Stein M, Rees G, Hicks L and Gorin S (2009) *Neglected Adolescents: A review of the research and the preparation of guidance for multi-disciplinary teams and a guide for young people*, DCSF-RBX-09–04, London: DCSF

Stevenson O (2007) *Neglected Children and their Families*, Oxford: Blackwell

Stringer B (2009) *Communicating through Play: Techniques for assessing and preparing children for adoption*, London: BAAF

Tanner K and Turney D (2000) 'The role of observation in the assessment of child neglect', *Child Abuse Review*, 9, pp 337–348

Taylor J and Daniel B (2005) *Child Neglect: Practice issues for health and social care*, London: Jessica Kingsley Publishers

Thoburn J and members of the Making Research Count Consortium (2009) *Effective Interventions for Complex Families where there are Concerns about, or Evidence of, a Child Suffering Significant Harm*, C4EO Safeguarding Briefing 1, London: C4EO

Turnell A and Edwards S (1999) *Signs of Safety: A solution and safety orientated approach to child protection*, London: Norton & Co

United Nations (1989) *Convention on the Rights of the Child*, adopted and opened for signature, ratification and accession by General Assembly Resolution 44/25, 20 November

Walker M (2005) *21st Century Review of Social Work: The statutory social worker's role in prevention and early intervention*, Stirling: University of Stirling Social Work Research Centre

Walker J (2008) 'The use of attachment theory in adoption and fostering', *Adoption & Fostering*, 32:1, pp 49–57

Ward H, Brown R, Westlake D and Munro ER (2010) *Infants Suffering, or Likely to Suffer, Significant Harm: A prospective longitudinal study*, DfE-RB053 Research Brief, London: DfE

Ward H, Munro ER and Dearden C (2006) *Babies and Young Children in Care: Life pathways, decision making and practice*, London: Jessica Kingsley Publishers

Winnicott D (1958) *Collected Papers*, New York, NY: Basic Books

Woodcock J (2003) 'The social work assessment of parenting: an exploration', *British Journal of Social Work*, 33:1, pp 87–106

Zeanah C (1996) 'Beyond insecurity: a reconceptualisation of attachment disorders in infancy', *Journal of Consulting and Clinical Psychology*, 64, pp 42–52